## High Scorer's Choice Series

# IELTS 5 Practice Tests

# Academic Set 1

## (Tests No. 1-5)

<u>High Scorer's Choice Series, Book 1</u>
**IELTS 5 Practice Tests, Academic Set 1 (Tests No. 1–5)**
**ISBN 9780987300928**
Copyright © 2017 Simone Braverman, Robert Nicholson.
First Edition April 2017
Updated August 2022

Available in print and digital formats
Accompanying audio recordings to be downloaded on the following webpage:
https://www.ielts-blog.com/ielts-practice-tests-downloads/

IELTS® is a registered trademark of University of Cambridge ESOL, the British Council, and IDP Education Australia, which neither sponsor nor endorse this book.

To contact the authors:
Email: simone@ielts-blog.com
Website: www.ielts-blog.com

<u>Acknowledgements</u>

The authors hereby acknowledge the following websites for their contributions to this book (see the webpage below for a complete list):

www.ielts-blog.com/acknowledgements/

While every effort has been made to contact copyright holders it has not been possible to identify all sources of the material used. The authors and publisher would in such instances welcome information from copyright holders to rectify any errors or omissions.

## Praise for
## High Scorer's Choice Practice Tests

*"I am a teacher from Australia. I had a Chinese friend who is studying for the exam and I used these [tests] to help him. I think the papers are very professional and useful. Many of the commercial practice papers are not culturally sensitive but this was not a problem with your tests."*
-   *Margaretta from Australia*

*"I found out that your practice papers are excellent. I took my IELTS on March 11th and got an Overall Band 8 with listening – 8, reading – 9, writing – 7 and speaking – 7. I spent one month on preparation."*
-   *Dr Yadana from London, UK*

*"I must tell you that the sample tests I have purchased from you have been the key to my preparation for the IELTS. Being employed full time I do not have the time to attend classes. I downloaded the material and made myself practice a few hours every 2 or 3 days for 3 weeks and was successful on my first trial. I was able to get an average of 7.5 and I was aiming at 7."*
-   *Oswaldo from Venezuela*

# High Scorer's Choice IELTS Books

## Academic    General

| | Academic | General | |
|---|---|---|---|
| Tests 1-5 | Set 1 | Set 1 | Tests 1-5 |
| Tests 6-10 | Set 2 | Set 2 | Tests 6-10 |
| Tests 11-15 | Set 3 | Set 3 | Tests 11-15 |
| Tests 16-20 | Set 4 | Set 4 | Tests 16-20 |
| Tests 21-25 | Set 5 | Set 5 | Tests 21-25 |
| Tests 26-30 | Set 6 | Set 6 | Tests 26-30 |

# CONTENTS

## Download Audio Content

In order to download the audio content please use a desktop computer (not a mobile device) with a reliable internet connection and open the following webpage in your browser:

**https://www.ielts-blog.com/ielts-practice-tests-downloads/**

Follow instructions on the webpage to save all audio files on your computer. The files are in mp3 format and you will need an audio player to listen to them (any modern computer has that type of software preinstalled).

# How to prepare for IELTS

There are two ways for you to use these practice tests for your exam preparation. You can either use them to work on your technique and strategy for each IELTS skill, or you can use them to simulate a real exam and make sure you will do well under time pressure.

**Option 1        Use practice tests to work on your IELTS skills (no time limits)**

To prepare well for the IELTS exam you need to have a strategy for each sub-test (Listening, Reading, Writing and Speaking). This means knowing what actions to take, and in which order, when you receive a test paper. If you are working with the IELTS self-study book "Target Band 7 – How to Maximize Your Score", all the necessary tips are located in the book. You need to read and then apply these tips and techniques when you are practicing on some of these tests. Don't time yourself, concentrate on learning the techniques and making sure they work for you.

If you purchased the practice tests in digital format, you will need to print out some pages, for easier learning and to be able to work in the same way as in the real test (on paper). Print the Listening questions and the Reading passages and questions. You can read the Writing and Speaking questions from your computer or mobile device, to save paper and ink. If you have the paperback format, this doesn't apply to you. Use Table of Contents on the previous page to navigate this book.

If Listening is one of your weaker skills, use transcripts while listening to recordings, when you hear words or sentences that you don't understand. Stop the recording, rewind, locate in the transcript the sentence you had a problem with, read it, and then listen to the recording again.

If Reading is hard for you, after doing the Reading test use the Reading Answer Help section of these practice tests to understand why the answers in the Answer key are correct. It will show you the exact locations of the answers in the Reading passages.

To compare your own writing to high-scoring samples go to Example Writing Answers and read them. Note the way the information is selected and reported in Writing Task 1, and the way an essay is organised in Writing Task 2.

To practice in Speaking, either read to yourself the Speaking test questions or get a friend to help with that. Record your answers and then listen to the recording. Note where you make long pauses while searching for the right word, pay attention to your errors and your pronunciation. Compare your own performance to that of students in sample interviews, and read their Examiner's reports.

**Option 2**       **Use practice tests to simulate the real test (strict time limits)**

This option will require some prep work before you can start a simulated test. Print out or photocopy the blank Test Answer Sheets for Listening and Reading and prepare some ruled paper on which to write your Writing Task 1 and 2. Also, think of a way to record yourself in the Speaking sub-test. Get a watch, preferably with a timer. Allocate 3 hours of uninterrupted time.

1. Be in a quiet room, put the Listening questions in front of you and start playing the recording. Answer questions as you listen, and write your answers next to the questions in the book.

2. When the recording has finished playing, allocate 10 minutes to transfer all your Listening answers to the Listening Answer Sheet. While you are transferring the answers check for spelling or grammatical errors and if you missed an answer, write your best guess.

3. Put the Reading passages and questions in front of you and set the timer to 60 minutes. Begin reading passages and answering questions. You can write the answers next to the questions or straight on the Answer Sheet. Remember that you don't get extra time to copy answers to the Answer Sheet, and that when 60 minutes are up all your answers must be written on the Answer Sheet.

4. Put the Writing questions in front of you and set the timer to 60 minutes. Make sure you don't use more than 20 minutes for Task 1, including proofreading time, and that you don't use more than 40 minutes for Task 2, with proofreading included.

5. Put the Speaking questions in front of you and begin the interview (remember to record your answers). In Part 2 take the whole 1 minute to prepare your speech and make notes, and then try to speak for 2 minutes (set the timer before you start talking).

6. When you have finished the whole test, take some time to rest, as you may be tired and it may be hard for you to concentrate. Then check your answers in the Listening and Reading against the correct ones in the Answer key, compare your writing tasks to the Example Writing tasks and your recorded speaking to the example interview. Analyse and learn from any mistakes you may find, and especially notice any problems with time management you may have encountered.

Remember, it is OK to make mistakes while practicing as long as you are learning from them and improving with every test you take.

Good luck with your exam preparation!

# PRACTICE TEST 1

## LISTENING

 Download audio recordings for the test here:
https://www.ielts-blog.com/ielts-practice-tests-downloads/

### PART 1      *Questions 1 – 10*

#### *Questions 1 – 5*

*Complete Angela's lost property form below.*

*Write **NO MORE THAN TWO WORDS AND/OR A NUMBER** from the listening for each answer.*

---

**Central Cinemas**
**Lost Property Form**

For the attention of:      Mr. Smith (responsible for lost property)

Customer's Name:      Peter (**1**) _____

Address:      (**2**) _____ Winchester Road
Alton

Postcode:      W12 (**3**) _____

Telephone:      Mobile: 01743 062 496

Film Watched:      *Spiderman*

Film Start Time:      (**4**) _____ p.m.

Seat (if known):      (**5**) _____

---

**Questions 6 – 10**

Choose *FIVE* letters, **A - L.**

What **FIVE** items does Peter's wallet contain?

**A**      Some business cards

**B**      Some money

**C**      A debit card

**D**      A note of PIN numbers for cards

**E**      Company identification

**F**      Company photocopy card

**G**      A cinema ticket

**H**      A theatre ticket

**I**       A hotel card key

**J**       A library card

**K**      A health insurance card

**L**      A passport

## PART 2          *Questions 11 - 20*

### *Questions 11 – 15*

*Below is a plan of the conference reception room with **11** locations marked (**A - K**). Questions **11 - 15** list 5 locations in and next to the conference reception room. Match the locations in questions **11 - 15** with the correct locations on the map and write the correct letter (**A - K**) next to questions **11 - 15**.*

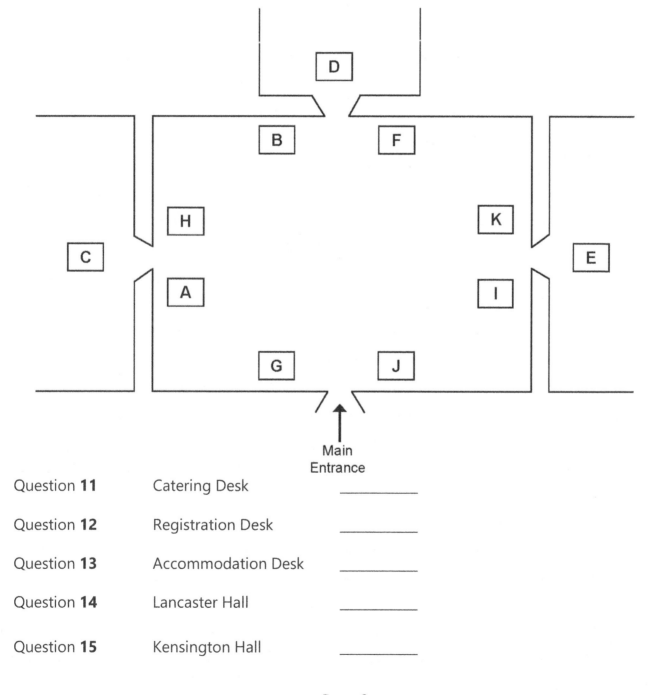

| | | |
|---|---|---|
| Question **11** | Catering Desk | _____ |
| Question **12** | Registration Desk | _____ |
| Question **13** | Accommodation Desk | _____ |
| Question **14** | Lancaster Hall | _____ |
| Question **15** | Kensington Hall | _____ |

## Questions 16 – 20

Answer the questions below. Write **NO MORE THAN THREE WORDS AND/OR A NUMBER** from the listening for each answer.

**16**    What food will be available on the tables in the mornings before the first speeches?

**17**    On what floor is the conference centre's restaurant?

**18**    How many choices of main course will there be at lunch for vegans?

**19**    Where will tea be served if the weather is good?

**20**    Where will Linda be found at lunch times?

## PART 3      Questions 21 – 30

### Questions 21 – 25

Complete the notes below. Write **NO MORE THAN THREE WORDS AND/OR A NUMBER** from the listening for each answer.

---

**Coastal Erosion Course**

**Locations**

Australia: Almost 36,000 km of coast with approx. (**21**) _____ made of sand. A lot of the course is focused here.

California: The Pacific threatens (**22**) _____ on the coastline here.

West Africa: Human factors - such as sand and gravel removal, and construction of ports, harbours and jetties (with dredging).

Natural factors - waves, tide, sea currents + winds ((**23**) _____ could affect these as well).

Others: UK, Louisiana and Hawaii.

**Field Trips**

Only in Australia. The main trip is to the Gold Coast and various (**24**) _____ there. Some trips are (**25**) _____. Lots of work and fun!

---

**Questions 26 – 30**

*Complete the table below.*

*Write* **NO MORE THAN TWO WORDS** *from the listening for each answer.*

| Type of Assessment | Number | Focus | Weighting |
|---|---|---|---|
| Essays | 6 | Different areas of the course. <br> Causes, (**26**) _____ and reactions. | 35% |
| Project | 1 | Students' choice - most choose an Australia topic. <br> Mostly (**27**) _____ choose an overseas topic. | 50% |
| Exam | 1 | (**28**) _____ long. Good knowledge of whole course expected. | 15% |
| * Only the (**29**) _____ can be re-done. Students are carefully selected and the (**30**) _____ try and spot students under-performing and help them. | | | |

## PART 4          *Questions 31 – 40*

*Questions 31 and 32*

*Complete the table below.*

*Write **NO MORE THAN TWO WORDS** from the listening for each answer.*

## Penguins

| Description | Flightless, but excellent swimmers. Body, feet, tail and flippers all aid swimming. Feathers are waterproof with woolly down and a deposit of (**31**)_____ underneath to keep them warm. |
|---|---|
| **Food** | Small fish + krill. |
| **Predators** | Leopard seals + (**32**) _____ in the sea; skuas and sheathbills on land. |
| **Classification** | Debated - 17 - 20 species of penguins. 4 species live on and around the Antarctic continent; the others in sub-Antarctic regions. |

*Questions 33 – 35*

*Choose the correct letter **A**, **B**, or **C**.*

33    The breeding sites for emperor penguins

   **A**    must be close to the sea.
   **B**    must be close to feeding grounds.
   **C**    must be on stable ice.

34    The egg of the emperor penguin

   **A**    is protected during incubation by the father.
   **B**    is protected during incubation by the mother.
   **C**    is protected on the feet of both the mother and the father.

35    The reason for the decline in numbers of emperor penguins at Pointe Géologie is

   **A**    due to the loss of ice there.
   **B**    unknown.
   **C**    due to warmer temperatures.

**Questions 36 – 40**

*Complete the summary below on the threats to emperor penguins.*

*Write **NO MORE THAN TWO WORDS AND/OR A NUMBER** from the listening for each answer.*

---

**Threats to Emperor Penguins**

The leopard seal is the principal predator of the emperor penguin, but birds can also eat eggs and young chicks, and (**36**) _____ reduces the emperor penguin's food source.

A less than (**37**) _____ Celsius upward change in temperature can cause changes in the Antarctic ice and could hinder 40 per cent of emperor penguins' attempts to find suitable (**38**) _____. The changes could cause a 20 per cent reduction in emperor penguin numbers.

Too much ice - greater distances to and from the sea to get food for the young and male.

Too little ice - (**39**) _____ can break up.

It's hoped that emperor penguins may adapt.

King penguins could displace emperor penguins, as they have a longer breeding season and survive better with less accessibility to (**40**) _____.

---

# READING

## READING PASSAGE 1

*You should spend about 20 minutes on **Questions 1 - 13**, which are based on Reading Passage 1 below.*

### Learning a Second Language

Various studies of second language learning have all shown that the benefits of learning a second language are much broader than simply the ability to speak in another language. Research affirms the importance of second language education regarding intellectual potential, scholastic achievement, first language skills, citizenship and the economy.

Learning a second language in this context is not learning a second language as a natural process when one acquires a first language. After childhood, the areas of the brain that are responsible for language acquisition become more fixed, and the process of picking up additional languages becomes more academic and less organic. The specific context concerns a person who has learned his or her first language automatically and is now learning a new language through a teacher, self-teaching or teaching oneself with a book or maybe online.

School children can get unexpected benefits from learning a foreign language. Educational research shows that results in English and Science are better for students who study one. The reasons for this are not altogether clear: perhaps the study skills acquired and used for studying another language also strengthen study skills used in other areas and it could also strengthen the ability to analyse and interpret information. It also seems that knowledge of the grammar of students' native language is often made clearer to them through explicitly learning another language's grammar. A foreign language is a whole new system with distinct rules, etymology, and meaning, which are just a few of the complexities of a language. Learning a new one puts the brain to task by recognising this new language structure. As the brain works out meaning and makes full use of this new arsenal to express ideas, it seems that it sharpens skills on reading, negotiating, and problem-solving.

Multi-tasking is stressful to those who are not skilled at it. People who are multilingual are proficient at slipping from one language system to another and using totally different language mechanics. This is very distracting and demanding work, not only for the tongue and language faculties, but also especially for the brain. People who have developed multilingual ability are highly proficient multi-taskers and commit very few errors when juggling various activities.

Related to this, with other factors held constant, several pieces of research have also shown that multilingual adults experienced the onset of Alzheimer's and dementia at a later age of 75 compared to monolingual adults, who had the first signs at age 71. The studies were conducted with other variables such as gender, overall health, educational level, and economic status, but there were no significant results that contributed to the mentioned diseases as significantly as the number of languages spoken. It seems that the more the brain is used, the better its functions work. Learning a new language structure entails familiarising with vocabulary and rules, and converting this memorised information into communication. This strengthens memory, because the brain has built its ability to associate information with mnemonics in order to retain information better. Hence, multilingual people have brains that are more exercised and quicker to recall.

Since a language is a doorway to a particular culture, learning a new language enables a person to have a broader understanding of the race or culture that speaks it. Opening up to a culture allows people to be more flexible and appreciative of other ways of doing and looking at things. As a result, if people are multilingual, they have the advantage of seeing the world from different vantage points. In today's interconnectedness, this is a valuable tool and with universal unemployment problems, a multilingual ability is definitely a competitive edge over others. Businesses are of course interested in people who have an ability that improves their intelligence, flexibility, openness to diverse people, and decision-making skills. And these are just bonuses to the evident ability to communicate in several languages and cross-cultural barriers. Additionally, speaking another language can simply give people a lot of pleasure, as they can communicate with others in their native language.

Finally, self-confidence is a normal consequence of learning a new language. By simply mastering one skill, the other faculties are developed. No matter their background, people tend to gravitate around multilingual people because of their skills; others simply find the openness and quick-mindedness of multi-lingual people naturally attractive. It is an interesting outcome, not at all something that is expected as a result when people embark to learn a new language, but trying to understand a language and the heritage that goes with it will put the learner in a position of self-discovery. It makes learners come to terms with how they view the world and other cultures, and have more appreciation of their own.

The cognitive and neurological benefits of learning a foreign language extend from early childhood to old age, as the brain more efficiently processes information and staves off cognitive decline. These cognitive and neurological benefits are instantly apparent, but there occurs a host of social, cultural and personal benefits, among them the ability to explore a culture through its native tongue or talk to someone with whom it might otherwise not be able to communicate. Learning a second language is best introduced at the earliest age possible, but learning it at a much later age is still very much worthwhile.

**Questions 1 – 5**

*Choose the correct letter **A**, **B**, **C** or **D**.*

*Write the correct letter in boxes **1 - 5** on your answer sheet.*

**1**    Studies have shown that second language learning can even affect

    **A**    a learner's health.
    **B**    a learner's life expectancy.
    **C**    a learner's ability in his or her mother tongue.
    **D**    a learner's stress levels.

**2**    The benefits that second language learning creates with children's study of other subjects

    **A**    are more noticeable in Mathematics.
    **B**    do not have fully understood reasons.
    **C**    are usually apparent in studies of children's first language.
    **D**    show themselves more in secondary school children.

**3**    Switching from one language to another

    **A**    is hard work for the brain.
    **B**    is not a natural process.
    **C**    can damage how the tongue shapes words.
    **D**    can cause confusion in older people.

**4**    The ability to switch from one language to another

    **A**    can lead to confusion when multi-tasking.
    **B**    can lead to mistakes when people do too many things at the same time.
    **C**    is unlikely to help people with the physical aspects of sport.
    **D**    helps people develop multi-tasking skills.

**5**    Bilingualism

    **A**    can delay the start of Alzheimer's disease.
    **B**    gives the same chance as anyone else of Alzheimer's disease after the age 71.
    **C**    means faster brain deterioration through more use than monolingualism.
    **D**    has been proved to have stopped Alzheimer's disease in some adults.

## Questions 6 – 9

*Do the following statements agree with the views of the writer of the text? In boxes **6 - 9** on your answer sheet write:*

| | |
|---|---|
| **YES** | *if the statement agrees with the writer's views* |
| **NO** | *if the statement doesn't agree with the writer's views* |
| **NOT GIVEN** | *if it is impossible to say what the writer thinks about this* |

**6**     Other health issues can affect an individual's likeliness to avoid Alzheimer's disease as much as second language abilities.

**7**     Studies have shown salaries are significantly higher for those people who are multilingual.

**8**     Multilingual people have a better ability to make decisions.

**9**     Multilingual people have longer life expectancies.

## Questions 10 – 13

*Complete each sentence with the correct ending (**A - G**) below. Write the correct letter (**A - G**) in answer boxes **10 - 13** on your answer sheet.*

**10**     An additional benefit of learning a second language

**11**     A successful second language learner

**12**     A society's traditions are better understood by a learner who

**13**     The time to learn a second language

**A**     does not have to be when a learner is young.

**B**     is something that cannot be experienced after approximately the age of 50.

**C**     is often instinctively appealing to those around him or her.

**D**     is that people feel better about themselves.

**E**     is a family experience that should not be avoided.

**F**     is open to study the society's language.

**G**     creates a severe feeling of inadequacy.

## READING PASSAGE 2

*You should spend about 20 minutes on* **Questions 14 - 26**, *which are based on Reading Passage 2 below.*

### Threats to the Great Barrier Reef

The Great Barrier Reef is well known as the world's largest system of coral reefs. Lying off the east coast of Australia, it covers an area larger than 300,000 square kilometres and is a unique habitat hosting billions of sea creatures. It also is a major source of income to people near the Reef, with tourism now being the key industry in the local towns.

Not all is well with the Great Barrier Reef; there are growing threats, the most serious being climate change. Organisations are working hard to impress upon the world's governments the need for urgent action to address climate change globally. To help boost the Reef's resilience to climate change, efforts are also being made to take action on the local effects of coastal development, such as from ports and agriculture.

Climate change threatens the Great Barrier Reef in different ways. Firstly, it can increase severe weather events, such as repeated cyclones and flooding. Cyclones can have devastating effects on the Great Barrier Reef, the immediate effect being the physical damage. Fast maturing coral is easily destroyed by storms, while slow maturing, more solid coral generally is spared. All coral though can be affected by the flooding caused by cyclones. Flooding on land can lead to large flood plumes from rivers being expelled into the sea that supports the Great Barrier Reef. Freshwater flood plumes can have a number of effects, including killing coral at shallow depths. Large scale flooding can carry various land-based pollutants, such as fertilisers, herbicides and the worst, pesticides, out to the Reef, which can have a devastating effect. A lesser-known problem is that earth or residue that is carried out to sea can affect coral growing in the deep water, as it can block out the light that coral needs to survive. In some locations, approximately 10 per cent of corals have bleached in shallow waters, indicating that the run-off is causing stress to reefs. Australian scientists have also observed sunken logs and terrestrial debris breaking up fragile corals in wave-exposed sections of the reefs. Although flood plumes are natural events, scientists predict that climate change worsens their impact. Expected increases in cyclone intensity will increase the size and frequency of flood events and thus the quantity of land-based runoff and pollutants making it to the Reef.

In the long-term, ocean acidification is likely to be the most significant impact of a changing climate on the Great Barrier Reef ecosystem. The oceans absorb carbon dioxide from the atmosphere and are estimated to have absorbed about half the excess carbon dioxide released by human activities in the past 200 years. This absorbed carbon dioxide is resulting in chemical changes in the ocean, which is referred to as ocean acidification. Although the chemistry is simple and well understood, its effect on marine life is much less well known, as the process has only been recognised for around a decade. Even relatively small increases in ocean acidity decrease the capacity of corals to build skeletons, which in turn decreases their capacity to create living environments for the Reef's marine life.

Climate change is also causing increases in sea surface temperatures and atmospheric temperatures. A lack of cloud cover and also freshwater run-off can all contribute to this. Temperature is a key environmental factor controlling the distribution and diversity of marine life; it is critical to reef building and controls the rate of coral reef growth more than anything. All animals and plants have temperature limits and when these are exceeded, natural processes break down. On coral reefs, surface temperature changes affect the relationship of mutual dependence between some animals and the algae that live within their tissues. The temperature gradient along the Great Barrier Reef has shifted markedly over the last century and is likely to continue to rise over the present century. Whatever climate scenario is used, it is predicted that by 2035, the average sea surface temperature will be warmer than any previously recorded.

Rising sea levels are another significant danger, because much of the Great Barrier Reef coastline is low-lying. Predictions of a future increase in sea levels are highly variable, but large changes in sea levels can mean land inundation, which will cause significant changes in tidal habitats, such as saltwater intrusion into low-lying freshwater habitats like mangroves. Sea levels on the Great Barrier Reef have already risen by approximately three millimetres per year since 1991, due to a combination of thermal expansion in the oceans and, most significantly, glaciers melting. Changes in sea levels from temperature increases are time-dependent and uncertain, because they are partly linked to the collapse of the Earth's great ice shelves. Reefs will probably be able to accommodate a sea level rise of three millimetres, however, as the rate of sea level rise increases, the Reef's coral will be more and more affected.

It seems that local people are motivated to change in order to protect the Great Barrier Reef, however, the worst threats to the Reef are because of climate change issues. As long as this continues, the Great Barrier Reef will continue to be in danger and with many countries in the world refusing to take action that might threaten their economies, it does not really matter how behaviours are changed in Australia.

Glossary

| | |
|---|---|
| Flood plume | A body of water that spreads out in a feather shape |
| Inundation | Flooding |

## Questions 14 – 20

*Look at the different results of climate change (questions **14 - 20**) and match them to the effects they have (**A - G**).*

*Write your answers in boxes **14 - 20** on your answer sheet.*

<u>Results of Climate Change</u>

**14**   Cyclones

**15**   Fresh water plumes

**16**   Sediment in the water

**17**   Ocean acidification

**18**   Rising ocean surface temperatures

**19**   Significant changes in sea levels

**20**   A sea level rise of only 3 millimetres


**A**   Ocean organisms have a smaller habitat, as coral growth can be hindered.

**B**   Few or no negative consequences will take place in reefs.

**C**   Coral growing in shallow water can be killed.

**D**   Freshwater ecosystems will be damaged by sea water.

**E**   Damage can occur to coral that grow quickly.

**F**   The reliance of certain organisms on each other can be affected.

**G**   Coral in deeper water die due to a lack of sunlight.

**Questions 21 – 26**

*Answer the questions below.*

*Write **NO MORE THAN THREE WORDS** from the text for each answer.*

*Write your answers in boxes **21 - 26** on your answer sheet.*

**21**     What contributes most to the economies of towns next to the Great Barrier Reef?

**22**     Which is the most dangerous agricultural pollutant that can be taken to the Great Barrier Reef through flooding?

**23**     For how long has it been known that ocean acidification has been taking place?

**24**     What is the most important influence on the growth of coral in the Great Barrier Reef?

**25**     What has been the key factor leading to sea levels rising in the Great Barrier Reef?

**26**     Who are interested in making changes to help protect the Great Barrier Reef?

## READING PASSAGE 3

*You should spend about 20 minutes on **Questions 27 - 40**, which are based on Reading Passage 3 below.*

### The Power of Music

Of the estimated sixty billion broadcast advertising hours encountered by North Americans each year, approximately three-quarters employ music in some manner.

Since the Ancient Greeks, music has been recognised as a powerful emotional force. They believed that music was such a powerful force that it could stir men into bravery on the battlefields or it could impose moral order and civilising harmony on unruly pupils. The rhythms and melodies of music can help words to stick in the brain much more effectively than if those words were delivered as speech alone, and music can also convey a particular mood.

By the twentieth century, music's emotional force was irresistible to advertisers, who wanted to influence their audiences into buying their products. Mass advertising using soundtracks began in the 1920's and 1930's with commercial radio in the United States, and, by the 1950's, most radio advertisements included an advertising jingle, which would help promote the products.

Music has also been central to television advertising since the 1950's, particularly because music can convey an emotional or subliminal message. A recently-published book describes how music was used in a TV commercial to sell Ford cars in 1959. Ford wanted to sell a particular car as an economy model, and they wanted to point out to potential buyers that it would actually save them lots of money on miles per gallon and other money-saving features. However, they worried that this might make the vehicle be perceived as low quality. To avoid this, the advertisers accompanied the advertisement with a soundtrack using lush string music, not usually associated with low price items, and the sales rocketed. The advert was judged a massive success because of the high quality subliminal message given by the music.

Music can serve the overall promotional goals in one or more of several capacities. Good music can contribute to the effectiveness of an advertisement merely by making it more attractive. A good advertisement engages the attention of an audience, and the most straightforward way of achieving this is to make it entertaining. Music serves to engage listeners' attention and render the advertisement less of an unwanted intrusion.

Music may also be employed in various structural roles. Perhaps the most important structural role is in tying together a sequence of visual images and/or a series of dramatic episodes, narrative voice-overs, or a list of product appeals. Historically originating in film music, advertising music can also be structurally employed as simply an uninterrupted background, or to heighten or highlight dramatic moments.

A third important function for music is to intensify the familiarity of a product. Consumers are known to favour products that elicit some degree of memory, even if it is merely the product's name. It is one of the peculiarities of human audition and cognition that music tends to linger in the listener's mind. Surprisingly, such musical lingering may occur even when the mind is an unwilling host. Thus, the association of music with the identity of a certain product may substantially aid product recall.

A fourth technique of musical enhancement is the use of lyrical language. Vocal music permits the conveyance of a verbal communication in a non-spoken way. Language utterances can sound much less naive or self-indulgent when couched within a musical phrase rather than being simply spoken. An individual can respectably sing things that would sound utterly trite if said.

Last is the use of music to enhance an advertisement's credibility and authority. Indeed, it may be the case that effective targeting is merely the result of the formation of proper authority. A simple way of creating this is through specialist testimony or employing celebrities. However, over periods of time, consumers become resistant to the means by which advertisers establish authority. One sophisticated way of getting round this is through music. Musical authority can be established most readily through quotation, allusion, or plagiarism.

The role of music in advertising recognises that music is a really powerful tool for selling things and this success has created added responsibilities to those people who wish to become music composers. From the middle of the twentieth century, composers have increasingly had to face extreme constraints if they have written music for films or TV or other media. In the 1930's, the rise of films with soundtracks led to a new type of commission for composers, where they had to tailor their music to a film scenario, to its narrative pace, and to the emotions of a character. They had to write music that was of a precise length, down to the nearest second, and more recently, film and TV composers have written so-called library music, where their soundtrack is categorised by describing its emotional evocation, and can be used in a variety of programmes. Viewers may have had the experience of watching a television programme and thinking, "I actually recognise that music from a previous series or a completely different programme." This is because the programme is using this so-called library music, where a composer has written music that is supposed to represent joy or the sun rising, and that music will then be reused whenever the producer of a film or a TV programme enters those particular emotional keywords into the database of library music.

However one measures good music, it must be acknowledged that, on a second-for-second basis, music created for the media, and especially for advertising, is perhaps the most meticulously crafted music in history. Nationally produced television advertisements in particular may be considered among the most highly polished cultural artifacts ever created. Whether this is ethical or not is an altogether different question.

## Questions 27 – 29

*Do the following statements agree with the information given in the text?*

*In boxes 27 – 29 on your answer sheet write:*

| | |
|---|---|
| **TRUE** | *if the statement agrees with the information* |
| **FALSE** | *if the statement contradicts the information* |
| **NOT GIVEN** | *if there is no information on this* |

**27**    One civilisation felt that music could help create stability with school children.

**28**    Music was not used in US radio advertising until the 1930's.

**29**    Complaints were made about the Ford Company's manipulative use of music in their advertising.

## Questions 30 – 36

*Complete the table below.*

*Write **NO MORE THAN TWO WORDS** from the text for each answer.*

*Write your answers in boxes 30 - 36 on your answer sheet.*

| Music's Roles in Advertising | |
|---|---|
| Entertainment | * Music can increase an advertisement's (**30**) _____ – it makes it more attractive and therefore engaging.<br>* Music can prevent the advertisement becoming an unwelcome (**31**) _____. |
| Structure | * Music can merge various media images or episodes.<br>* Music can create a continuous setting.<br>* Music can emphasise (**32**) _____. |
| Recall | * Music can increase a product's (**33**) _____.<br>* Music can remain in a subject's memory, even when the target subject is (**34**) _____. |
| Lyrical Beauty | * Music can make a spoken message's conveyance sound more meaningful and less silly than if it were spoken. |
| Credibility | * This is often done in advertising by establishing authority using experts or (**35**) _____.<br>* (**36**) _____, however, become accustomed and resist this.<br>* Music can create authority in different ways. |

## Questions 37 – 40

*Complete the summary using the words in the box below.*

*Write your answers in boxes **37 - 40** on your answer sheet.*

---

### Music's Influence in Advertising on Composers

Music's influence in advertising has led to added (**37**) _____ for aspiring composers. Since music has been written for the media, composers have been faced with restrictions. Music has to undergo (**38**) _____ to the media's different requirements. Library music is collected to present any (**39**) _____ that is required and therefore viewers can hear the music in different media. The right music for a situation can be accessed in a database using a particular (**40**) _____ that expresses the needed emotion.

---

| | |
|---|---|
| destruction | mood |
| adjustment | study |
| observation | pressure |
| term | program |

# WRITING

## WRITING TASK 1

*You should spend about 20 minutes on this task.*

**The bar chart below shows the average rainfall for Australia by month for last year. The line shows the average rainfall for Australia by month for the last 40 years.**

**Summarise the information by selecting and reporting the main features, and make comparisons where relevant.**

*You should write at least 150 words.*

### Average Rainfall for Australia for Last Year by Month

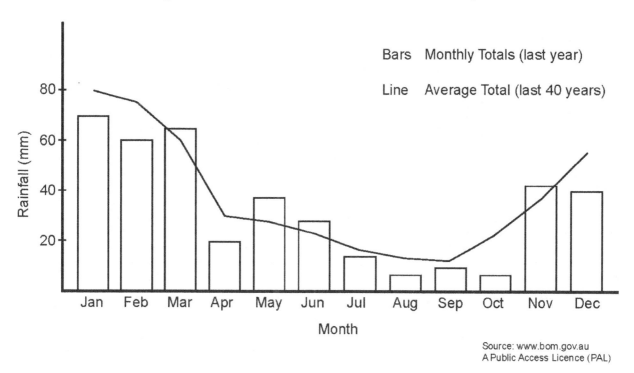

## WRITING TASK 2

*You should spend about 40 minutes on this task.*

*Write about the following topic:*

> **Today's schools should teach their students how to survive financially in the world today.**
>
> **To what extent do you agree or disagree with this statement?**

*Give reasons for your answer and include any relevant examples from your knowledge or experience.*

*You should write at least 250 words.*

# SPEAKING

## PART 1

- Can you tell me a little about where you live?
- Which is your favourite room in the house/flat where you live?
- What changes would you like to make to where you live?

Topic 1       Fruits and Vegetables
- Do you like fruits and vegetables? What fruits and vegetables are popular in your country?
- Why are fruits and vegetables so good for people?
- How can we get young people to eat more fruits and vegetables?
- Do you think you could ever be a vegetarian? (Why/Why not?)

Topic 2       The Weather
- What are the typical seasonal weather conditions in your country?
- How do you think weather can affect people's moods?
- Do you feel weather patterns are changing nowadays? (Why?)
- What do people like to do in your country when it's raining?

## PART 2

Describe your ideal car. You should say:
      what kind of car you'd like
      what special features you'd like it to have
      where you'd like to travel in it
and explain why it would be your ideal car

## PART 3

Topic 1       The Advantages and Disadvantages of Cars
- What are some of the advantages and disadvantages of owning a car?
- Do you think cars should be banned from city centres? (Why/Why not?)
- What other measures can governments introduce to stop people using cars so much?
- How do you feel that cars will be improved over the next 50 years?

Topic 2       Driving and the Law
- At what age should be people be allowed to start driving and what age should they stop? (Why?)
- What are the laws like regarding driving speeds in your country?
- What laws does your country have about driving and alcohol?
- Do you feel there should be a law about how long one can drive without stopping?

# PRACTICE TEST 2

## LISTENING

 Download audio recordings for the test here:
https://www.ielts-blog.com/ielts-practice-tests-downloads/

### PART 1          Questions 1 – 10

**Questions 1 – 5**

*Answer the questions below. Write* **NO MORE THAN THREE WORDS AND/OR A NUMBER** *from the listening for each answer.*

**1**     In what month is Katherine's birthday?

**2**     What is Katherine's last name?

**3**     At what time would Katherine like the party to start?

**4**     What activity is not available on the chosen date?

**5**     How many people will Katherine invite to the party?

## Questions 6 – 10

*Complete the information sheet and price list for John's outdoor center below.*

*Write* **NO MORE THAN TWO WORDS AND/OR A NUMBER** *from the listening for each answer.*

---

**John's outdoor centre**

Opening Times:     Monday – Friday      7 a.m. – 8 p.m.
                            Saturday & Sunday  8:30 a.m. - (**6**) _____ p.m.


Price List

| | | |
|---|---|---|
| Activities | Bonfire | $15 |
| | Boat Tour | $(**7**) _____ per person |
| | Cycling Tour | $8 per person |
| | Hiking Tour | $25 per person |
| | Baking (15 people max) | $(**8**) _____ per person |
| | | |
| Food & Drinks | Small Buffet | $200 |
| | Large Buffet | $(**9**) _____ |
| | Lamb on a Spit | $35 |
| | | |
| Staying Overnight | Camping with Tents | $40 per tent (4 people per tent) |
| | Tipi | $80 per tipi (20 people per tipi) |
| | Tree House | $(**10**) _____ (20 people) |

---

## PART 2      *Questions 11 - 20*

### *Questions 11 – 14*

*Below there is a map of the town of Barton with the locations of features of interest (**A - T**) of Sharon's walking tour marked on it. Match the locations in questions **11 - 14** with the correct locations on the map and write the correct letter (**A - T**) next to questions **11 - 14**.*

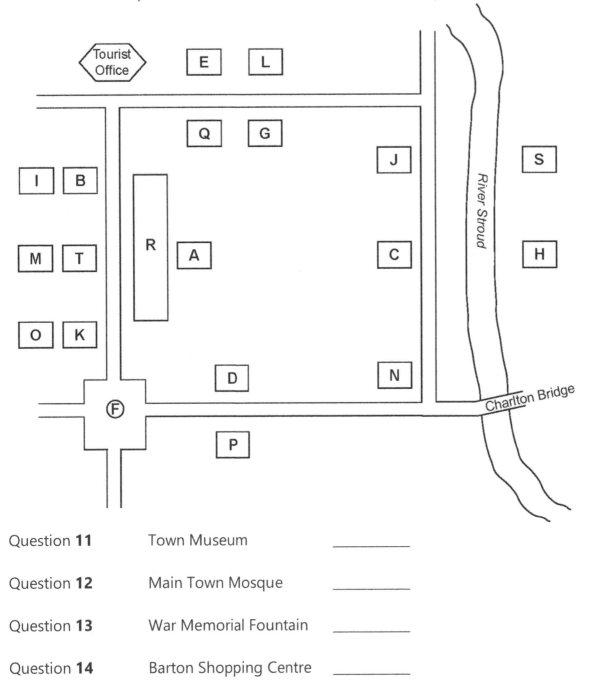

| Question **11** | Town Museum | _____ |
| Question **12** | Main Town Mosque | _____ |
| Question **13** | War Memorial Fountain | _____ |
| Question **14** | Barton Shopping Centre | _____ |

**Questions 15 and 16**

*Choose the correct letter **A**, **B**, or **C**.*

**15**     For how long does Sharon estimate her walking tour of the town will last?

     **A**     2½ hours

     **B**     2 hours + 20 minutes

     **C**     3 hours

**16**     How much does Sharon charge for her walking tour of the town?

     **A**     20 pounds

     **B**     5 pounds

     **C**     Nothing

**Questions 17 – 20**

*Choose **FOUR** letters, **A** - **H**.*

What **FOUR** things does Sharon say people can do that evening in Barton?

**A**     Watching live music

**B**     Watching live football

**C**     Watching films

**D**     Going on a tour of the town's theatre

**E**     Watching a play at the town's theatre

**F**     Taking part in a quiz

**G**     Watching some theatre performed in the town square

**H**     Watching tennis on television

## PART 3    Questions 21 – 30

**Questions 21 – 25**

*Complete the table below.*

*Write **NO MORE THAN ONE WORD** from the listening for each answer.*

| Students' Agriculture Project Progress | | |
|---|---|---|
| *Student* | *Project* | *Notes* |
| Steve | How parasites affect the growth rates of potatoes. | * Steve interacted with (**21**) _____ to gather his data.<br>* Steve had to rent a (**22**) _____ himself to gather data on growth with parasites.<br>* Steve sold his potatoes and made a profit. |
| Simone | A study of the speed of (**23**) _____ for different tomato varieties. | * Simone used a university greenhouse to use for growing the tomatoes. |
| Robert | Initially wanted to examine how the (**24**) _____ of soil affects plant growth, but due to a late start he switched to the growing techniques used by apple farmers. | * The apple project had better success due to the later (**25**) _____.<br>* Robert visited many apple growers near his parents' house. |

**Questions 26 – 30**

*Complete the sentences in the notes below.*

*Write **NO MORE THAN TWO WORDS AND/OR A NUMBER** from the listening for each answer.*

Projects <u>MUST</u> be submitted as a (**26**) _____ to Professor Evans by the 28th February and by email to Mrs. Roberts by the (**27**) _____. Mrs. Roberts' email address is in the course literature, website and on the dept. noticeboard.

Word limit is increased this year by (**28**) _____ words (now 10,000, not including the (**29**) _____).

Prof. Evans' advice should stop projects from failing, but if they aren't good enough, the failing student will not (**30**) _____. The project can be redone (or a new one done) the next year.

## PART 4    *Questions 31 – 40*

### *Questions 31 – 35*

*Choose the correct letter **A**, **B**, or **C**.*

**31**    The Rorschach Test was initially based on

    **A**    how schizophrenics see things differently.

    **B**    schizophrenics self-analysis of themselves.

    **C**    observation of the schizophrenic child of a well-known psychologist.

**32**    The Rorschach Test uses

    **A**    a unique method in how it assesses people.

    **B**    a common method to assess people.

    **C**    a method that is nowadays very infrequently administered to assess people.

**33**    The Rorschach ink blots are

    **A**    first shown to subjects the day before the test.

    **B**    first shown to subjects an hour before the test.

    **C**    not supposed to be ever made public before the test.

**34**    The accuracy of the Rorschach Test

    **A**    has been demonstrated through careful experimentation.

    **B**    is now largely discredited.

    **C**    is widely used in the United States.

**35**    Interpretation of the Rorschach Test's results

    **A**    is still disputed among psychologists and psychiatrists using the test.

    **B**    is now universally done using the Exner Comprehensive System.

    **C**    are often confirmed using modern personality tests.

**Questions 36 – 40**

*Complete the sentences below.*

*Write* **NO MORE THAN TWO WORDS** *from the listening for each answer.*

36     In the Exner Comprehensive System, the structural summary results are meant to demonstrate _____ associated with the different responses given.

37     The rigidity of method used when delivering the Rorschach Test is supposed to keep _____ in results to a minimum.

38     The person delivering the Rorschach Test will rarely provide any _____ to the test taker.

39     Nowadays, the tests are recorded, but in the past, a particular _____ was created for people to write notes during the Rorschach Test.

40     Efforts are made to stop test takers becoming _____ or distracted, as this can create unreliable results.

# READING

## READING PASSAGE 1

*You should spend about 20 minutes on* **Questions 1 - 13**, *which are based on Reading Passage 1 below.*

### The Story of the Battery

When people consider today how indispensable the Internet is, they often overlook that without electricity, it would not function. Living without the Internet would be a significant inconvenience today, but without electricity, life as we know now it would collapse. Since we started using electricity, which was in the middle of the nineteenth century, we have worked on ways to move and store it easily and efficiently and one of the most common ways of storing electricity has been the battery. A battery does not actually store electricity. A battery, which is actually an electric cell, is a device that produces electricity from a chemical reaction. The story of the battery is one of people trying to create different compounds to create an electric current. The two goals on improving batteries have always been to create ones that can produce an electric current for a long time and to make them smaller and smaller.

Alessandro Volta is credited with creating in 1800 the first battery and the first practical method of generating electricity. Luigi Galvani, another Italian scientist and contemporary of Volta, almost made the discovery, but misinterpreted his research results. Using a frog's leg in an experiment, Galvani concluded that the electric current was 'animal electricity' and did not come from the apparatus he had set up. Volta's battery was made by piling up layers of silver and paper or cloth, soaked in salt, and zinc. These layers were assembled, without paper or cloth between the zinc and silver, until the current was created.

Volta's battery was not good for delivering currents for any significant duration. This restriction was overcome in the Daniell Cell in 1820. Using different chemicals, John Daniell used a copper pot, copper sulphate, sulphuric acid and mercury to produce his electric current. Although we now know better than to put mercury into batteries, this battery, which produced about 1.1 volts, was used to power telegraphs, telephones, and even to ring doorbells in homes for over 100 years.

Although many other chemical combinations were used in batteries over the years, the lead acid battery is one that stands out. First made in 1859, it was further improved in 1881 and this design even now forms the basis of the modern lead acid battery found in cars.

One very common battery used today is the lithium-ion battery, which was developed by the United States' Central Intelligence Agency (CIA) as a part of their efforts during the Cold War. The idea surrounding the lithium-ion battery was to create a power source that could provide a long-duration, high-density energy supply in a small package. In the early 1960's, both the private and public sectors were experimenting with creating batteries using lithium, but the breakthrough in the chemistry was achieved by adding the ion into the equation. Not long after its invention, the CIA shared the lithium-ion battery concept with the public and a company working on an exploratory project developed and created the first patent for the lithium-ion battery for commercial use in 1968. Used for a variety of different applications, the first lithium-ion battery was a game-changer in the medical industry, where it is used as the power source in heart pacemakers.

Today, the lithium-ion battery is the most common type of battery used in pacemakers, because of its reliability and life span. Most lithium-ion batteries can last 10 years or longer in a cardiac pacemaker. What makes lithium-ion batteries even more valuable in cardiac pacemakers is that, when the battery nears the end of its life, the voltage begins to decrease. Because of the battery's decreasing voltage, electrical designers can design an indicator for the pacemaker that allows the device to inform the doctor a new battery is needed. The battery can then be changed safely before it completely discharges. Lithium-ion batteries can also be used for other medical applications, including neurostimulation and insulin pumps for diabetics.

Whilst people consider the mid-nineteenth century to have been when civilisation started using electricity, there has been a discovery of what could be a battery that seems to indicate that electricity was used long ago. What has become known as the Parthian Battery was found on a railway construction site in 1936. Dating back 2,000 years, the 'battery' would have comprised a clay jar filled with a vinegar solution. An iron rod was put into the middle of the jar and encircled with copper wire. Tests have shown that this 'battery' could produce 2 volts of electricity. It would have not been used for electricity as we generally use it today, but it has been theorised it could have been used for electroplating objects with metals, such as gold or silver. Most scientists reject these theories nowadays and hypothesise that the 'battery' was more likely to have been used for the storage of scrolls.

Although battery research is proceeding at a steady pace, with an average annual gain in capacity of six per cent, what scientists are hoping for is that a battery will be developed that can last even longer and be lighter and smaller. One completely different technology that is being explored is to create a battery that can power a house; size would not be such an issue, but its generating capacity and length of life would have to be something totally different from what we have yet experienced.

## Questions 1 – 5

*Complete the table below.*

*Write **NO MORE THAN TWO WORDS** from the text for each answer.*

*Write your answers in boxes **1 - 5** on your answer sheet.*

| Some Older Batteries | |
|---|---|
| **Battery** | **Notes** |
| Volta's Battery | * Invented in 1800<br>* Beat his contemporary, Galvani, who made errors with his (**1**) _____<br>* Used silver, paper or cloth, salt and zinc in (**2**) _____<br>* Not good for long (**3**) _____ |
| Daniell's Battery | * Made using different chemicals<br>* Used (**4**) _____, which is not used any more<br>* Produced just over 1 volt and was used for over 100 years |
| The Lead Acid Battery | * A significant development from 1859 that still is used in (**5**) _____ today |

## Questions 6 – 10

*Complete the sentences below.*

*Write **NO MORE THAN TWO WORDS** from the text for each answer.*

*Write your answers in boxes **6 - 10** on your answer sheet.*

**6**     The lithium-ion battery was invented as part of the United States' contribution to the _____.

**7**     The _____ that allowed the success of the lithium-ion battery was the chemical addition of the ion to the equation.

**8**     A _____ for creating the lithium-ion battery commercially was only possible when the CIA shared its work publically.

**9**     The lithium-ion battery is used a lot in pacemakers due to its _____ and how long it keeps its charge.

**10**    Developments in the lithium-ion batteries for pacemakers allowed an _____ to be included to show when the battery needs to be replaced.

## Questions 11 – 13

*Label the diagram below.*

*Write **NO MORE THAN THREE WORDS** from the text for each answer.*

*Write your answers in boxes **11 - 13** on your answer sheet.*

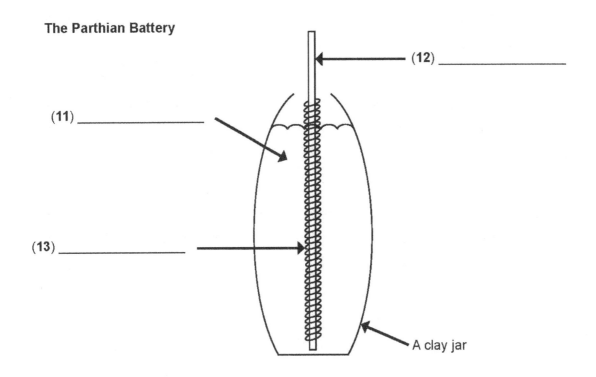

**The Parthian Battery**

(12) _____

(11) _____

(13) _____

A clay jar

## READING PASSAGE 2

*You should spend about 20 minutes on **Questions 14 - 26**, which are based on Reading Passage 2 below.*

### Can All Reading Help Children?

It is generally acknowledged that reading is an important part of a child's learning process. Reading is a way for children to make connections between what they already know and what they see around them. These connections help children understand the world they are in, and, through books, children are exposed to characters and cultures that they may not otherwise interact with in real life.

A recent debate has examined what kinds of reading are best for children and whether any type of reading is beneficial. Many children are attracted to one genre or type of book, or they may have a favourite author that they like to read time and time again. Even though children may enjoy reading a single type of literature, they can be gently introduced to other genres. 'Gently' is important, because parents or teachers do not want to push too hard and run the risk of turning the child off reading. So, why is it important for children to read a variety of books and stories? Primary school teacher, Carol Anderson explains that there are several good reasons. "The exposure to different authors and genres of books can give your child insight into other societies, worldwide locations, and new vocabulary." Child-specific genres also provide a key link from the present to the past. Anderson again explains. "These genres are often stories that are passed down from generation to generation and they can be fascinating. Folk tales, fairy tales, fables, legends and myths, while retaining much of their original flavour and content, have to evolve in subtle ways to remain meaningful in different eras. They are a great starting point to introduce children to the concept of a story and to introduce them to different types of stories or genres."

But is all reading good? There is so much written that is done so badly and with questionable content. But if those are the only books a reluctant reader will pick up, do their drawbacks outweigh the benefit of having the student finally turning pages? "I think you should be glad they're reading anything at all," says Patricia Edwards, distinguished professor of language and literacy at Michigan State University. In her area of specialisation of creating home reading environments for families, she has become accustomed to the reality that there are often not typically strong reading role models for students at the end of the day. "A lot of parents don't have reading as a tradition and there aren't any books they would suggest their children read. So if a student gravitates toward a book, even if it's not a classic from the literary canon, that shouldn't be cause for alarm."

Joining her in the any-reading-is-good camp is Deborah Wooten, a board member of the Children's Literature Assembly. Children learn how language and writing work, even when reading books dismissed by some as piffle, says Wooten. Wooten is also concerned with other issues. "There is decreased readership among children and young adults because of digital distractions." To prove her point, she cites a recent study that showed teenagers spend roughly four hours a night in front of a television or computer.

But plenty of parents put themselves in the opposite camp. Don Croft, a parent of a six-year-old boy, recently wrote in an online review of a book that he saw his child reading, that he had to stop after every other sentence and talk about how his child should not follow the examples he read about in this particular book. "I had to point out that we don't call people stupid, we don't judge others by the fact that you can beat them up, and you don't deal with being afraid by calling everyone names and hitting them."

Librarian, Mike Howard, disagrees. "The books that we believe to be poor quality may introduce students to reading. After they are hooked with these books, it is our job as educators and parents to slowly begin introducing new books to these students. As long as the students are able to develop the skill of visualising what they are reading, they are learning." Another point of view is that 'low quality literature' can give the opportunity to teach a child to be a critical thinker and that parents can use the child's interest as a springboard for recommendations for other, more substantive literature. Author, Judy Blume, who has had her books banned by various organisations, feels that parents worry too much about their children's reading material. "If a book is really unsuitable, the children themselves will simply self-censor themselves." Although Blume has sold over 80 million of her books worldwide, she still finds people critical of what she has written. "A lot of people want to control everything in their children's lives, or everything in other people's children's lives."

Reading for pleasure is an activity that has real consequences in the life of a child. There is a growing body of evidence that emphasises the importance of reading for pleasure, for both educational purposes as well as personal development. The evidence strongly supports the argument that those who read more are better readers and do significantly better at school. Children who read very little do not have the benefits that come with reading, and studies show that when struggling readers are not motivated to read, their opportunities to gain knowledge decrease significantly. Whether any type of reading can be considered beneficial is moot and it probably lies with parents and teachers to lay down their own beliefs in guiding children's reading patterns.

Glossary

Piffle – nonsense or rubbish

## Questions 14 – 21

*Look at the following statements (questions 14 - 21) and the list of people below.*

*Match each statement with the correct person's initials.*

*Write the correct initials in boxes 14 - 21 on your answer sheet.*

**14**    Some books provide unsuitable role models.

**15**    Some adults are motivated to interfere in all aspects of children's lives.

**16**    Different book types can teach children about different cultures.

**17**    Reading books has been affected by modern media usage.

**18**    Too many children don't have parental role models who read.

**19**    Different types of children's literature is a good starting point for children to learn about how stories work.

**20**    If reading can induce the process of imagination, then it is a valuable learning experience.

**21**    Children can learn about how language functions, even from poorly written books.

| | |
|---|---|
| **CA** | Carol Anderson |
| **PE** | Patricia Edwards |
| **DW** | Deborah Wooten |
| **DC** | Don Croft |
| **MH** | Mike Howard |
| **JB** | Judy Blume |

## Questions 22 – 25

Complete the sentences below.

Write **NO MORE THAN TWO WORDS** from the text for each answer.

Write your answers in boxes **22 - 25** on your answer sheet.

22    Poor books can also teach a child to be a _____, as he or she recognises
      what is bad.

23    Children have the ability to _____ their reading if they find it inappropriate.

24    Reading for enjoyment can have a significant impact on children's educational and
      _____ growth.

25    Children who miss out on reading a lot can find their _____ for learning are
      considerably diminished.

## Question 26

Choose the correct letter, **A, B, C or D**.

Write the correct letter in box **26** on your answer sheet.

26    What is the writer's purpose in Reading Passage 2?

      **A**    To discuss which genres are best for child readers.
      **B**    To explain what reading parents and teachers should help children avoid.
      **C**    To discuss whether all reading can be beneficial for children.
      **D**    To explain how reading is beneficial for children.

## READING PASSAGE 3

*You should spend about 20 minutes on **Questions 27 - 40**, which are based on Reading Passage 3 below.*

### The Spanish Influenza Pandemic of 1918

The Spanish influenza pandemic of 1918 to 1919, which caused around 50 million deaths worldwide, remains an ominous warning to public health.

**Paragraph A**

Before and after 1918, most influenza pandemics developed in Asia and spread from there to the rest of the world more or less simultaneously. Historical data are inadequate to identify the geographic source of the 1918 virus. The name 'Spanish' influenza merely reflects that Spain, which was neutral in World War 1, did not censor their news agencies from publicising the severity of the pandemic in the country, and this made it seem to other countries that the disease was worse there.

**Paragraph B**

The pandemic did not occur evenly over 1918 and 1919, but came in three severe waves. The first, or so-called spring wave, began in March 1918 and spread unevenly through the United States, Europe, and possibly Asia over the next six months. Illness rates were high, but death rates in most locales were not appreciably above normal. A second or autumn wave spread globally from September to November 1918, was highly fatal and, in many nations, a third wave occurred in early 1919. Clinical similarities led contemporary observers to conclude initially that they were observing the same disease in the successive waves. The differences between the waves seemed to be primarily in the much higher frequency of complicated, severe, and fatal cases in the last two waves. These three extensive pandemic waves of influenza within one year, occurring in rapid succession, with only the briefest of quieter intervals between them, were unprecedented.

**Paragraph C**

All of these deaths caused a severe disruption in the US economy. Claims against life insurance policies skyrocketed, with one insurance company reporting a 745 per cent rise in the number of claims made. Small businesses, many of which had been unable to operate during the pandemic, went bankrupt. The world economy as a whole was not significantly affected and the 1920's actually heralded a growth boom, until the 1929 Wall Street Crash. The US had a great influence on world economics and, although over 650,000 people died in the US, it could have been a lot worse. Throughout history, influenza viruses have mutated and caused pandemics or global epidemics. In 1890, an especially virulent influenza pandemic struck, killing many Americans. Those who survived that pandemic and lived to experience the 1918 pandemic tended to be less susceptible to the disease and so a lot more Americans lived than would have otherwise been the case.

**Paragraph D**

In the years following 1919, people seemed eager to forget the pandemic. Given its devastating impact, the reasons for this forgetfulness are puzzling. It is possible, however, that the pandemic's

Page 45

close association with World War I may have caused this short memory. While more people died from the pandemic than from World War I, the war had lasted longer than the pandemic and caused greater and more immediate changes in American society. Influenza hit areas quickly and often, but it disappeared within a few weeks of its arrival. Many people did not have time to fully realise just how great the danger was.

**Paragraph E**
The 1918 Spanish Influenza pandemic had some curious features. Firstly, overall, nearly half of the influenza-related deaths in the 1918 pandemic were in young adults of 20 to 40 years of age, a phenomenon unique to that pandemic year. The 1918 pandemic is also unique among influenza pandemics in that the absolute risk of influenza death was higher in those under 65 years of age than in those over 65. Influenza is usually more dangerous for the very young and the old, as their immune systems are weaker. Secondly, the pandemic was particularly widespread during the summer and autumn, whilst usually influenza is more widespread in the colder winter months. Finally, in 1918, three separate recurrences of influenza followed each other with unusual rapidity, resulting in three explosive pandemic waves within a year's time.

**Paragraph F**
The 1918 Spanish Flu pandemic was particularly fatal with more than twice the fatalities of World War 1. Scientists today have isolated the virus and researched why it was so particularly lethal. The theory is that it often killed through an over-stimulation of people's immune systems, a process known as a cytokine storm. This is when there is an overproduction of immune cells and associated compounds to fight an infection. As the infection was influenza, the cells congregated in the lungs, and their large numbers led to inflammation followed by secondary bacterial pneumonia. This secondary disease was the cause of the many deaths, particularly in healthy young adults, because of their robust immune systems that could produce so many cytokines. Ironically, the health of the young adults made them the most affected.

**Paragraph G**
In its disease course, the 1918 pandemic was different in degree, but not in kind, from previous and subsequent pandemics, including Covid-19. Despite the extraordinary number of global deaths, most influenza cases in 1918 were mild and essentially indistinguishable from influenza cases today. Although laboratory experiments on influenza genes from the 1918 virus suggest that the 1918 and 1918-like viruses seem to be as sensitive as other typical virus strains to today's anti-influenza drugs and even with today's prevention knowledge, the return of a pandemic virus similar to the virus of 1918 would likely kill over 100 million people worldwide, as the ease of travel in today's globalised society would aid the movement of the virus. Fortunately, Covid-19 was not as deadly as the 1918 influenza virus. However, although some characteristics of the 1918 pandemic appear unique, scientists have concluded that, since it happened once, similar or more favourable conditions could lead to another equally devastating pandemic.

Glossary

A pandemic – a disease active over the whole world or over a country.
Epidemiology – the science of the origins, spread and control of a disease.

## Questions 27 – 33

*The text on the previous pages has 7 paragraphs (**A – G**).*

*Choose the correct heading for each paragraph from the list of headings below.*

*Write the correct number (**i – x**) in boxes **27 – 33** on your answer sheet.*

| | |
|---|---|
| **i** | Out of Mind |
| **ii** | Economic Effects |
| **iii** | Inadequate Vaccines |
| **iv** | Origins of the Name |
| **v** | The Risks Today |
| **vi** | The Course of the Pandemic |
| **vii** | A Famous Doctor |
| **viii** | Unusual Aspects |
| **ix** | Why so Deadly? |
| **x** | Influenza in the War Zone |

**27**      Paragraph A

**28**      Paragraph B

**29**      Paragraph C

**30**      Paragraph D

**31**      Paragraph E

**32**      Paragraph F

**33**      Paragraph G

## Questions 34 – 37

*Choose the correct letter **A, B, C or D**.*

*Write the correct letter in boxes **34 - 37** on your answer sheet.*

**34**     Spanish influenza received its name because

    **A**       it was first diagnosed in Spain.

    **B**       Spain's soldiers coming home from World War 1 were the most severely affected.

    **C**       the Spanish media publicised the effects more.

    **D**       a Spaniard first transferred the virus to the United States.

**35**     The attack of the virus in three waves

    **A**       had never been experienced before.

    **B**       allowed doctors to treat the later cases more effectively.

    **C**       led to the government learning from previous mistakes.

    **D**       meant sickness was most severe at the start.

**36**     The 1918 Spanish influenza pandemic

    **A**       indirectly led to great prosperity in the 1920's.

    **B**       had a severe effect on the world economy in the following years.

    **C**       had no appreciable influence on the world economy.

    **D**       indirectly led to the 1929 Wall Street Crash.

**37**     A previous influenza pandemic

    **A**       meant that the United States had more fatalities than expected in the 1918 Spanish influenza pandemic.

    **B**       led to many Americans surviving the 1918 Spanish influenza pandemic.

    **C**       meant many Americans caught the 1918 Spanish influenza virus more easily.

    **D**       was brought to the United States from South America.

## Questions 38 – 40

*Do the following statements agree with the information given in the text?*

*In boxes **38 – 40** on your answer sheet write:*

> **TRUE**           *if the statement agrees with the information*
> **FALSE**        *if the statement contradicts the information*
> **NOT GIVEN**    *if there is no information on this*

**38**    Because Spanish influenza was often only active for a short time in some communities, its impact was not always appreciated.

**39**    The 1918 Spanish influenza virus was first identified in Asia.

**40**    The very young, sick and old were more at risk from the 1918 Spanish influenza pandemic.

# WRITING

## WRITING TASK 1

*You should spend about 20 minutes on this task.*

**The pie charts below show the amount of electricity generated by energy source in Scotland for 20 years ago and last year.**

**Summarise the information by selecting and reporting the main features, and make comparisons where relevant.**

*You should write at least 150 words.*

**Amount of Electricity Generated in Scotland, by Energy Source for 20 Years Ago**

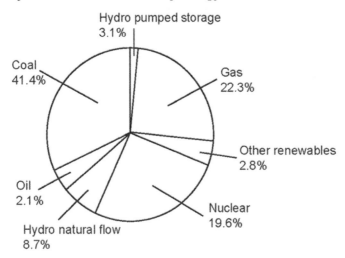

**Amount of Electricity Generated in Scotland, by Energy Source for Last Year**

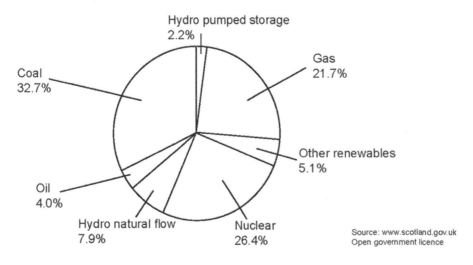

Source: www.scotland.gov.uk
Open government licence

## WRITING TASK 2

*You should spend about 40 minutes on this task.*

*Write about the following topic:*

**Some people today believe that the world's increase in population is unsustainable and will eventually lead to a global crisis. Other people believe that world population increase is necessary and beneficial as it creates the growth of the world's economy and society.**

**Discuss both these views and give your opinion.**

*Give reasons for your answer and include any relevant examples from your knowledge or experience.*

*You should write at least 250 words.*

# SPEAKING

## PART 1

- Tell me about the outside of your house or apartment building.
- What can the outside of a building say about who lives there?
- What would you change to the outside of your house or apartment building?

Topic 1        Public Transport
- Do you use public transport? (Why/Why not?)
- How could public transport be improved where you live?
- Can you compare the bus and train as types of public transport?
- How can governments get people to use public transport more?

Topic 2        Films
- What kinds of films do you like and what kinds do you dislike?
- What can people learn from watching films?
- Is there a successful film industry in your country? (Why/Why not?)
- How have films changed since you started watching them?

## PART 2

Describe a memorable holiday that you once took.
You should say:
        where this holiday was
        who you went with
        what you did during this holiday
and explain why this holiday was so memorable.

## PART 3

Topic 1        The Holiday Industry
- Where do people from your country like to go on holiday?
- Why do people need holidays?
- Can you compare the holiday industry today with that of 30 years ago?
- What problems can tourists create in holiday resorts?

Topic 2        Moving to Another Country/Emigration
- Would you ever consider living permanently in another country other than your own? (Why/Why not?)
- Why do people choose to move to other countries?
- What problems do people face when they move to other countries?
- How do you think emigration patterns will change over the next 50 years?

# PRACTICE TEST 3

## LISTENING

 Download audio recordings for the test here:
https://www.ielts-blog.com/ielts-practice-tests-downloads/

### PART 1        *Questions 1 – 10*

*Questions 1 – 5*

*Complete Tom's Existing Customer Enquiry Form below.*

*Write* **NO MORE THAN THREE WORDS AND/OR A NUMBER** *from the listening for each answer.*

**Existing Customer Enquiry Form**

| | |
|---|---|
| Contract Number: | TR349573 |
| Date of Birth: | 12th March (**1**) _____ |
| Zip Code: | 85823 |
| House Number: | (**2**) _____ |
| Customer's Name: | Jennifer (**3**) _____ |
| Home Telephone: | 01934 (**4**) _____ 342 |
| Monthly Bill Paid By: | (**5**) _____ |

## Questions 6 – 10

*Complete Jennifer's notes below.*

*Write **NO MORE THAN TWO WORDS AND/OR A NUMBER** from the listening for each answer.*

---

Tom, the sales guy at R&N Mobile, said I would not get the extra (**6**) _____ of internet that I wanted, and he was able to issue a new contract, as the (**7**) _____ had not been activated yet. The new deal has no extra costs and also gives access to the fast TFR Network.

I can still terminate the contract as long as I do it (**8**) _____ days in advance. The price of US$(**9**) _____ per month has not changed.

If I want to get a new cell phone, I can order one on the website - Tom will send me the (**10**) _____ to the online store by email. I had to sign to reauthorize my payment.

---

## PART 2      *Questions 11 – 20*

*Questions 11 – 15*

Choose **FIVE** letters, **A - O**.

*Which of the following can be found in the Johnson Building?*

**A**      Central coffee bar

**B**      The pizzeria

**C**      The French bistro

**D**      Asian street café

**E**      The main reception

**F**      The finance office

**G**      The maintenance team office

**H**      The first aid centre

**I**      The cinema

**J**      The doctor's surgery

**K**      The Fitness Area

**L**      The saunas

**M**      The steam rooms

**N**      The main swimming pool

**O**      The Internet café

**Questions 16 – 20**

*Complete the table below.*

*Write **NO MORE THAN THREE WORDS AND/OR A NUMBER** from the listening for each answer.*

| Activity | Time | Notes |
|---|---|---|
| Water Park Complex | 9 a.m. - 6 p.m. | £10 public.<br>Reserved for holiday park (**16**) _____<br>from 9 a.m. to 12 noon. |
| Mini-golf | 9 a.m. - 6 p.m. | All equipment supplied; groups play at<br>(**17**) _____ intervals. No cost. |
| Jogging | 8 a.m. or 5 p.m. | Morning jog easier - flat + (**18**) _____ km<br>approx. in length.<br>Afternoon jog harder - hillier + 6 km in length.<br>Both runs begin with gentle (**19**) _____<br>and finish with stretching. |
| Levington Excursion | Minibus departs park<br>at 1 p.m. + departs<br>Levington at 5 p.m. | Costs £2; buy at reception or from the<br>(**20**) _____; book early to avoid<br>disappointment |

## PART 3     Questions 21 – 30

### Questions 21 – 25

*Choose the correct letter **A, B, or C**.*

**21**    What is the subject of Professor Norris' seminar next week?

   **A**    History

   **B**    China

   **C**    The students' next essay

**22**    What is Alex's course about?`

   **A**    How wild boar were re-introduced in the UK

   **B**    How animals breed in different environments

   **C**    How foreign species of animal affect environments

**23**    What was most responsible for reducing the numbers of UK wild boar until they totally disappeared in the thirteenth century?

   **A**    Disease

   **B**    Too much hunting

   **C**    A royal order for their extermination

**24**    What was the main problem with farming wild boar in the UK in the 1970s?

   **A**    It did not make much money

   **B**    The animals kept escaping

   **C**    Hunters killed the animals

**25**    Why is the number of boar now probably more than 800?

   **A**    More and more boar have escaped from farms

   **B**    The escaped and released boar have bred

   **C**    The Forestry Commission has released more boar to ensure healthy bloodlines

## Questions 26 – 30

*Complete the summary below on the wild boars of the Forest of Dean.*

*Write **NO MORE THAN TWO WORDS** from the listening for each answer.*

---

### The Wild Boars of the Forest of Dean

The wild boars of the Forest of Dean are now officially wild animals and the local (**26**) _____ is responsible for them.

Many locals say the high numbers of boars is not a problem. It's reported that the (**27**) _____ will move the young away when they meet humans. Males are more aggressive, but only dogs have been chased.

The Forestry Commission now regularly kills boars to control numbers, but animal rights activists attempt to disrupt the (**28**) _____ working in the forest doing this.

The forest cannot be closed on cull days and activists patrol the (**29**) _____ where they know the culls take place to protect the animals. The forest rangers are upset, saying the boars create an imbalance in the forest. The rangers now try and kill the wild boars on (**30**) _____ dates.

---

## PART 4    *Questions 31 – 40*

### *Questions 31 – 34*

*Complete the notes below.*

*Write **NO MORE THAN THREE WORDS AND/OR A NUMBER** from the listening for each answer.*

---

**The New Zealand's Exclusive Economic Zone (EEZ)**

New Zealand's EEZ is 5th largest in the world - covers approx. 3.9 million km².

New Zealand's EEZ's depth can be up to **(31)** _____ metres.

Underwater landscape of New Zealand's EEZ includes mountains, valleys, geysers + mudflats. Much marine life grows there.

Fishing can damage sea life, especially with bottom trawl or dredge equipment.
      Factors include:      Type of seabed habitat
                            The specialised **(32)** _____ used

**Bottom-Trawling**

Possibly the most destructive fishing type. Involves large nets being dragged over sea floor that take everything.

The unwanted species taken (called the **(33)** _____) are thrown back in sea, often dead or dying. This can be up to 90% of each trawl.

Conservationists claim sea floor life takes a long time to recover, if at all. This is disputed by **(34)** _____.

---

**Questions 35 – 37**

*Choose the correct letter **A, B, or C**.*

**35**     Part of New Zealand's fisheries management program is likened to

**A**     similar initiatives in other countries.

**B**     similar initiatives on land.

**C**     similar initiatives that were not implemented in the past.


**36**     Most current BPA seabeds

**A**     have never had trawlers operating there.

**B**     have been carefully charted by the New Zealand Ministry of Fisheries.

**C**     have been damaged by previous fishing.


**37**     Charted hydrothermal vents

**A**     are difficult to locate for protection purposes.

**B**     are key targets for the fishing industry.

**C**     are closed to all fishing.


**Questions 38 – 40**

*Complete the sentences below.*

*Write **NO MORE THAN THREE WORDS AND/OR A NUMBER** from the listening for each answer.*

**38**     It's claimed that more than _____ per cent of the New Zealand EEZ has never been subject to bottom trawling.

**39**     Conservation critics of the New Zealand government claim that not all vulnerable _____ are protected.

**40**     The work of industrial trawlers also affects the _____ of smaller communities, as the catches of their fishermen also suffer.

# READING

## READING PASSAGE 1

*You should spend about 20 minutes on **Questions 1 - 13**, which are based on Reading Passage 1 below.*

### The Life of Marie Curie

Marie Curie was a remarkable woman from Poland whose discoveries broke new ground in physics and chemistry, and also opened the door for advances in engineering, biology, and medicine. She was the first woman to receive a doctor of science degree in France, the first woman to win the Nobel Prize, the first woman to lecture at the Sorbonne, the first person to win two Nobel Prizes, and the first Nobel Laureate whose child also won a Nobel Prize. Her life offers insights into the changing role of women in science and academia over the past century.

Although Marie's family was not wealthy, both parents were teachers and instilled in their children a love of learning and a deep patriotism, which led to her opposing the Russian occupation of her country. At the time of her birth, Poland was not an independent country and Warsaw was in the part of Poland that was under the control of Russia. Czar Alexander II, the then ruler of Russia, hoped to stamp out Polish nationalism by keeping the people ignorant of their culture and language, and schools were strictly controlled. Although Marie did very well in her school studies, her early days did not show any startling characteristic to indicate that one day she would become the most famous woman scientist in the world.

Marie, along with her sister, Bronya, started attending the Floating University. The name 'Floating University' derived from the fact that it was an illegal night school and its classes met in changing locations to evade the watchful eyes of the Russian authorities. It was obvious that the education given by the Floating University could not match the education provided by any major European university. Both Marie and her sister nurtured a hope of going to Paris to study at the Sorbonne University, however, their father was not in a position to send them to Paris for higher studies. Both the sisters realised that individually, they did not have enough resources to enable them to go to Paris, so they decided that one of them would go first by pulling their resources together. Bronya went first, as she was the older sister and they agreed that Bronya would fund Marie after her graduation as a doctor. Marie worked several years as a governess to finance her older sister's studies at the Sorbonne. In 1890, Bronya graduated and a year later, Marie began her university degree in Paris. At graduation, one of two women in a graduating class of several thousand, Curie ranked first in physics.

After graduation, Marie returned to Poland, as she intended to work there and care for her father. However, she was persuaded by fellow scientist Pierre Curie to return to Paris. Pierre wrote, "It would be a beautiful thing if we could spend our lives near each other. Hypnotized by our dreams - your patriotic dream, our humanitarian dream and our scientific dream." Pierre and Marie married and began their historic collaboration on the nature of radioactivity at a small institute out of the mainstream of the scientific establishment.

In 1896, Becquerel had shown that uranium compounds, even if they were kept in the dark, emitted rays that would fog a photographic plate. This was an accidental discovery, as he was trying to find out whether the new radioactivity discovered by Roentgen could have a connection with fluorescence. The scientific community initially ignored Becquerel's intriguing finding. Marie, however, decided to make a systematic investigation of the mysterious uranium rays for her doctorate degree. Marie found that two uranium minerals, pitchblende and chalcocite, were more active than uranium itself, so she hypothesised that a new element that was considerably more active than uranium was present in small amounts.

Working in the small institute with Pierre, Marie had an independence she might not have had at the Sorbonne, where she probably would have been expected to elaborate some superior's work. In their joint work, Pierre observed the properties of the radiation, while Marie purified the radioactive elements. By July 1903, they had isolated a new element, and they wrote, "We propose to call it polonium after the name of the origin of one of us." Soon they had isolated another new element, radium. Both the new elements were much more radioactive than uranium and their discoveries brought the Curies international fame with the awarding of the Nobel Prize in 1903.

Following Pierre's death in a road accident in 1906, Marie's status changed again. Now she was a celebrated woman of accomplishment without a husband to make the celebrity acceptable. Marie was appointed as a professor at the Sorbonne University, but her application for membership in the Academy of Sciences in 1910 was rejected, and there can be little doubt she was refused because she was a woman. After this humiliation, Marie became involved in a romantic scandal, but, in spite of public outrage and the objections of some members of the Swedish Academy, Marie received her second Nobel Prize in 1911.

Over the next 20 or so years, Marie worked with radioactive elements and, because the dangers of working with them were not fully understood at that time, the long exposure led to her sickness and death from a type of leukaemia at the age of 66. The amount of radiation she was exposed to is shown by the fact that her old papers and even her cookbook from a hundred years ago are still too dangerous to handle without specialised protective clothing.

## Questions 1 – 7

*Complete the notes below.*

Write **NO MORE THAN THREE WORDS** *for each answer.*

*Write your answers in boxes **1 - 7** on your answer sheet.*

---

### The Life of Marie Curie

* Marie's achievement for a scientist and a woman were unprecedented and changed people's views about the developing (**1**) _____ in her academic field.

* Marie's parents made her a successful student in Russian-controlled Warsaw; due to her (**2**) _____, she was against the Russian occupation.

* Although attending the Floating University with Bronya, they both wanted to study at the Sorbonne. Lacking the (**3**) _____ for both their studies, Bronya studied first and, after becoming a doctor, paid for Marie's studies. Marie came first in her class.

* Marie married Pierre Curie after graduation and decided to take a doctorate and study (**4**) _____, which had recently been discovered by Roentgen. Marie wanted to search for what she believed was a new element in the (**5**) _____ where uranium was found.

* With the help of her husband, Marie discovered polonium and radium, the former named after her (**6**) _____. Marie and Pierre won the Nobel Prize.

* After Pierre died, Marie became a professor at the Sorbonne, was refused entry to the Academy of Sciences, was involved in a scandal and won her second Nobel Prize.

* Marie's (**7**) _____ to radioactivity all her working life led to her dying of leukaemia when she was 66.

---

### Questions 8 – 13

*Look at the different significant years in Marie Curie's life (questions **8 - 13**) and match them to the events that took place in those years (**A - F**).*

*Write your answers in boxes **8 - 13** on your answer sheet.*

Significant Years in Marie Curie's Life

**8**     1891

**9**     1896

**10**    1903

**11**    1906

**12**    1910

**13**    1911

**A**     Marie's attempt to join the Academy of Sciences was blocked.

**B**     Marie received her second Nobel Prize.

**C**     Becquerel discovered that rays from uranium affected photographic plates by accident.

**D**     Marie and Pierre won the Nobel Prize for physics.

**E**     Marie began her studies at the Sorbonne.

**F**     Pierre died.

## READING PASSAGE 2

*You should spend about 20 minutes on **Questions 14 - 26**, which are based on Reading Passage 2 below.*

### Tidal Energy

Tidal energy is a form of hydropower that utilises large amounts of power within the ocean's tides to generate electricity. Tidal energy is a renewable energy source, as the Earth uses the gravitational forces of both the moon and the sun everyday to move vast quantities of water around the oceans to produce tides.

There are different kinds of tidal power systems. A tidal barrage is a type of tidal power generation that involves the construction of a fairly low dam wall, known as a 'barrage', across the entrance of a tidal inlet or basin, creating a tidal reservoir. This dam has a number of underwater tunnels cut into its width allowing seawater to flow through them in a controllable way, using a sluice gate on the sea and reservoir side, which can slide down or up to release or retain water as desired. Fixed within the tunnels are propellers that are turned by the tidal flow and they in turn spin a turbine. The movement creates a magnetic field within the generator above, which is converted to electricity.

One disadvantage of tidal barrage electricity generation is that it can only generate electricity when the tide is actually flowing either in or out, as during high and low tide times the tidal water is stationary. However, as the tides are completely predictable, it is straightforward to plan how to compensate for low generation times with other providers in the energy mix. Supporters of tidal power also point out that other renewable energy resources, such as solar and wind farms, are much more unpredictable and intermittent. Other disadvantages of a tidal barrage system are the high construction costs and the environmental effects that a long concrete dam may have on the estuary it spans.

A tidal stream generation system reduces some of the environmental effects of tidal barrages by using turbine generators beneath the surface of the water. Major tidal flows and ocean currents, like the Gulf Stream, can be exploited to extract their tidal energy, using underwater rotors and turbines. Tidal stream generation is very similar in principal to wind power generation, except this time, water currents flow across a turbine's rotor blades that rotate the turbine, much like how wind currents turn the blades for wind power turbines. In fact, tidal stream generation areas on the seabed can look just like underwater wind farms.

Unlike offshore wind power turbines, which can suffer from storms or heavy sea damage, tidal stream turbines operate just below the sea surface or are fixed to the seabed. Tidal streams are formed by the horizontal fast flowing volumes of water caused by the ebb and flow of the tide, as the profile of the seabed causes the water to speed up as it approaches the shoreline.

As water is much denser than air and has a much slower flow rate, tidal stream turbines have much smaller diameters and higher tip speed rates compared to an equivalent wind turbine. One of the disadvantages of tidal stream generation is that, as the turbines are submerged under the surface of the water, they can create hazards to navigation and shipping.

A good example of a successful tidal power project is the La Rance power station in France. This tidal barrage is still the largest tidal power station in the world, in terms of installed capacity, with a peak rating of 240 megawatts generated by its 24 turbines, and an annual output of approximately 600 gigawatts. The building expenditure was significant, even back in 1966 when it was opened, but these have now been recovered and electricity production costs are lower than that of nuclear power. The high cost of tidal barrages, however, is what has discouraged the further construction of similar projects.

The environment at La Rance has remained healthy, but there have been changes. The barrage has caused limited silting of the Rance ecosystem, although this has been manageable. Sand eels and plaice have reduced in numbers, but sea bass and cuttlefish have returned to the river. The tidal flows are regulated in the estuary by the operators, who adjust them to minimise the biological impact.

The La Rance tidal plant produces a source of energy that is clean, renewable and sustainable. It has no impact on climate, because it does not emit any greenhouse gases. The pattern of the tides is preserved, so that the impact on species living in the estuary is minimal. The operator monitors the tides and weather forecasts to program the barrage operations on a weekly basis.

Since the construction of the barrage, a new ecological equilibrium has been established in the Rance estuary and there is an abundance of fish, bird and other wild life. The water levels in the lagoon are higher than it was before the construction, which has promoted an increase in boating and sailing activities. The facility attracts approximately 70,000 visitors per year and a lock in the west end of the dam permits the passage of 20,000 vessels each year between the English Channel and the Rance.

Tidal power offers society a clean and renewable source of energy. Although technology is still at a relatively immature stage, economic projections indicate that tidal energy could become cost-competitive over the long-term and governments should explore potential sites for taking advantage of these natural opportunities.

## Questions 14 and 15

*Label the diagram below.*

*Write **NO MORE THAN THREE WORDS** from the text for each answer.*

*Write your answers in boxes **14 and 15** on your answer sheet.*

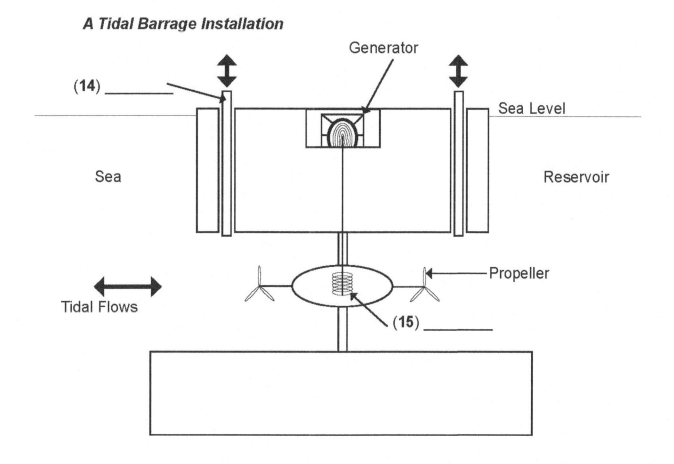

**A Tidal Barrage Installation**

## Questions 16 – 19

*Complete each sentence with the correct ending (**A - F**) below. Write the correct letter (**A - F**) in answer boxes **16 - 19** on your answer sheet.*

**16** A problem with tidal barrages is

**17** Less impact on the environment is

**18** The generation of tidal stream energy is

**19** The higher density of the water that passes through tidal stream turbines is

**A** created by projects with a tidal stream energy source rather than tidal barrage projects.

**B** their potential for negative impact on the area behind the dam.

**C** much more expensive than fossil fuel installations.

**D** one reason the turbines that are rotated are smaller.

**E** not a popular choice with local people and governments.

**F** largely the same process used with another renewable power source.

## Questions 20 – 26

*Complete the summary below.*

*Write **NO MORE THAN TWO WORDS** from the text for each answer.*

*Write your answers in boxes **20 - 26** on your answer sheet.*

---

### The La Rance Tidal Barrage

Built in 1966, the La Rance Tidal Power Station is the world's largest tidal barrage. The considerable (**20**) _____ on construction has been recovered and it's now more efficient than (**21**) _____. Negative environment effects have been limited and (**22**) _____ are controlled to reduce problems. The zero emissions don't affect the (**23**) _____ and wildlife is little affected. Knowledge of tides and (**24**) _____ helps this. The estuary ecology has changed, but sometimes for the better. The higher (**25**) _____ has led to increases in tourism and a (**26**) _____ regulates busy water traffic through the barrage.

---

# READING PASSAGE 3

*You should spend about 20 minutes on **Questions 27 - 40**, which are based on Reading Passage 3 below.*

Is imprisonment the solution to crime? With soaring crime rates being made up mostly of re-offenders, people are questioning the effectiveness of prisons and whether there are viable options to replace or work in conjunction with them.

There seems to be confusion as to what exactly prison is for. Prison director, Katherine Soames, has mixed feelings about her establishment's purpose. "Some say prison is for punishment, but prison is an oblique and expensive way of punishing people. Heavy fines would surely give back more to society than having them languish in a cell. Some say deterrence is the main factor, but there is little evidence of such an effect. Hardened criminals do not fear prison and short prison sentences are probably counterproductive in that they operate as 'schools for crime'. As for rehabilitation, prisons stigmatise people, sever family ties and make it more difficult to get employment on release."

Another reason sometimes given for putting people in prison is retribution, the argument being that people should 'have to pay for what they have done'. Unfortunately, this often penalises people for the consequences of their behaviour, regardless of whether harm was intended. If a driver falls asleep at the wheel and causes the death of ten people, he has no more criminal intent than if he hit a tree and injured himself. He is not dangerous after his driving licence has been taken away, but a man was recently sentenced to five years in prison for this. Prosecutor Angela Martin comments on this case. "While prison might please the relatives of those killed, it is unnecessary for the protection of society and expensive to the taxpayer. I believe the only proper use of prison is for the containment of dangerous criminals, including violent men and serial burglars who cannot be reformed."

Can prison be of use at rehabilitation? Ministry of Justice executive, Colin Case, explains some facts. "Recidivism figures give little cause for optimism regarding the effectiveness of short- or medium-term prison sentences. Ministry of Justice figures show that a crime is committed every 10 minutes by a criminal on bail." Other figures support Case. In the UK for example, one-third of those cautioned or convicted last year had at least 15 previous convictions and only ten per cent were first time offenders. One 66-year-old shoplifter had 330 convictions over fifty years and was still released immediately with a short prison sentence, because he had already served half of it while awaiting trial.

Can we predict in advance which criminals are likely to reoffend? Researchers have attempted to do so. Recently, a study measured impulse control while monitoring brain activity with an MRI. Error-related responses in the anterior cingulate cortex (ACC) indicative of impulsiveness were predictive of rearrest within the four years following release from prison. Those with low activity in the ACC were about twice as likely to be recidivists. The researcher in charge of the study, Sophie Meaker, comments on the results. "While our study gives us some data to help guide our actions with regard to reoffending, they are still not accurate enough for determining life-altering decisions with respect to individuals."

One possible more humane alternative to prison and one of the best is community service. This has elements of punishment (deprivation of freedom and some degree of humiliation), reparation (payback to the community) and rehabilitation (it maintains community ties and promotes a work ethic). Jason Howell, a judge in Australia, is a fan. "It is better than short-term prison sentences at reducing reoffending and allows monitoring without a prison sentence. It can take the pressure off the prison system, yet still enforce justice."

Another answer to the over-crowding and ineffectiveness of prison is to turn to electronic tagging, which is the attachment of a transmitter to an offender, usually to the ankle. A control centre can monitor the whereabouts and movements of anyone wearing a tag. This can and ought to be used as a sentence in itself or part of an early release system. It can enforce many of the benefits of prison by requiring offenders to be at home for certain specified hours of the day or night, without incurring the expense of running the prison.

John Dawson, a US child psychologist, explains one key benefit. "Electronic tagging can be of immeasurable benefit for young offenders. Instead of being sent to a young offenders' institute, where they might mix and learn bad habits from other offenders, they can remain in society with their families, and still be monitored. Many young people are very scared by the repercussions of what they have done and keeping them away from negative role models can be enough to allow them to avoid a life of crime."

Research has suggested that electronic tagging would create significant monetary savings, although so far, conclusions have only been based on extrapolating the results of limited trials. There has also been some criticism. Activist Tom Wilkinson argues that tagging should be illegal. "Tagging clearly contravenes a couple of basic human rights, such as the right not to undergo degrading treatment or the right to a private family life. Tagged prisoners have frequently complained of being stigmatised and treated like animals." Parole officer, Alison Headley, opposes tagging for almost an opposite reason. "Tagging is a soft option and one that most prisoners, especially re-offenders, would prefer. It does not punish sufficiently or effectively and does not discourage re-offending." When taking this into account, it seems that tagging is not a suitable measure for re-offenders.

Whatever one's point of view, finding the right solution to the punishment system in today's society is still open to debate. Prison will continue to be widely used, but there will be constant efforts to find alternatives that can punish effectively in an economic way.

Glossary

Recidivism – A return to criminal behaviour.
MRI – Magnetic resonance imaging.
Parole – The conditional release of a prisoner with certain agreed requirements.

### Questions 27 – 33

*Look at the following statements (questions **27 - 33**) and the list of people below.*

*Match each statement with the correct person's initials.*

*Write the correct initials in boxes **27 - 33** on your answer sheet.*

**27**     There is still not enough evidence to understand why criminals reoffend.

**28**     Prison should still be used for violent criminals.

**29**     Electronic tagging would often be the punishment of choice for many criminals.

**30**     Prison can severely affect family relationships for offenders.

**31**     Community service can be more effective than brief prison sentences at stopping people committing crimes after release.

**32**     Electronic tagging can be inhumane.

**33**     Reoffending statistics show that prison is ineffectual as a deterrent to committing crime.

| | |
|---|---|
| **KS** | Katherine Soames |
| **AM** | Angela Martin |
| **CC** | Colin Case |
| **SM** | Sophie Meaker |
| **JH** | Jason Howell |
| **TW** | Tom Wilkinson |
| **AH** | Alison Headley |

## Questions 34 – 39

*Do the following statements agree with the views of the writer of the text?*

*In boxes **34 - 39** on your answer sheet write:*

**YES**            *if the statement agrees with the writer's views*
**NO**             *if the statement doesn't agree with the writer's views*
**NOT GIVEN**      *if it is impossible to say what the writer thinks about this*

**34**    The purpose for the existence of prisons is unclear for some people.

**35**    One problem with community service is that it cannot impose the feeling of embarrassment for having committed a crime.

**36**    Researchers should study the reactions of prisoners to community service in order to measure its effectiveness.

**37**    Electronic tagging should not be a method for shortening a criminal's prison sentence.

**38**    Electronic tagging should not be an option for repeat offenders.

**39**    The use of prison in society will diminish.

## Question 40

*Choose the correct letter, **A, B, C or D**.*

*Write the correct letter in box **40** on your answer sheet.*

**40**    What is the best title for the text in Reading Passage 3?

    **A**    Prison – Still the Best Punishment
    **B**    Prison and its Alternatives
    **C**    UK Prison Life Today
    **D**    The Benefits of Electronic Tagging

# WRITING

## WRITING TASK 1

*You should spend about 20 minutes on this task.*

**The two tables below show statistics of workers of foreign and US birth in the United States last year.**

**Summarise the information by selecting and reporting the main features, and make comparisons where relevant.**

*You should write at least 150 words.*

| Analysis of Last Year's United States' Workforce - Workers in the US of Foreign Birth<br><br>All Figures in Thousands | By Gender | Total in Workforce | Number of Employed | Number of Unemployed | Unemployment Rate - % |
|---|---|---|---|---|---|
| | Male | 14,385 | 13,643 | 1,284 | 8.9 |
| | Female | 9,972 | 8,326 | 1,104 | 11.1 |
| | *Totals* | *24,357* | *21,969* | *2,388* | *9.8* |
| | By Age | Total in Workforce | Number of Employed | Number of Unemployed | Unemployment Rate |
| | 16 - 24 | 1,975 | 1,661 | 314 | 15.9 |
| | 25 - 34 | 5,937 | 5,387 | 550 | 9.3 |
| | 35 - 44 | 6,884 | 6,265 | 619 | 9.0 |
| | 45 - 54 | 5,719 | 5,172 | 547 | 9.6 |
| | 55 - 64 | 3,011 | 2,727 | 284 | 9.4 |
| | 65 + | 831 | 757 | 74 | 8.9 |

| Analysis of Last Year's United States' Workforce - Workers in the US of US Birth<br><br>All Figures in Thousands | By Gender | Total in Workforce | Number of Employed | Number of Unemployed | Unemployment Rate - % |
|---|---|---|---|---|---|
| | Male | 67,610 | 60,414 | 7,196 | 10.6 |
| | Female | 61,923 | 56,682 | 5,242 | 8.5 |
| | *Totals* | *129,533* | *117,095* | *12,438* | *9.6* |
| | By Age | Total in Workforce | Number of Employed | Number of Unemployed | Unemployment Rate |
| | 16 - 24 | 18,960 | 15,417 | 3,543 | 18.7 |
| | 25 - 34 | 27,678 | 24,842 | 2,836 | 10.2 |
| | 35 - 44 | 26,482 | 24,398 | 2,084 | 7.9 |
| | 45 - 54 | 30,242 | 28,019 | 2,223 | 7.4 |
| | 55 - 64 | 20,286 | 18,909 | 1,377 | 6.8 |
| | 65 + | 5,886 | 5,511 | 375 | 6.4 |

## WRITING TASK 2

*You should spend about 40 minutes on this task.*

*Write about the following topic:*

> **Although the prices of fossil fuels have greatly increased over the last decade or two, it is argued that further increases in these fuel prices are the only way to reduce world consumption of fuel and lessen pressure on the world's fossil fuel resources.**
>
> **To what extent do you agree or disagree with this statement?**

*Give reasons for your answer and include any relevant examples from your knowledge or experience.*

*You should write at least 250 words.*

# SPEAKING

## PART 1

- Tell me a little about your country.
- What are some of the advantages and disadvantages of living in your country?
- Where would you advise a visitor to your country to visit? (Why?)

Topic 1      Libraries
- Do people in your country go to libraries? (Why/Why not?)
- What function do libraries have in communities?
- Do you feel that using a library should be free?
- Do you think libraries are a thing of the past or do you think they have a future?

Topic 2      Sports
- Do you play any sports? (Why/Why not?)
- What sport would you/did you encourage your child to play?
- Why do you think people like to watch sports?
- What is your attitude to high risk/dangerous sports?

## PART 2

Describe a memorable place that you have visited
You should say:
> where this place is
> when you first went there
> what you did there
and explain why this place is so memorable for you.

## PART 3

Topic 1      Cities
- Do you prefer to live in a city or in the countryside? (Why?)
- What are the advantages of living in a big city?
- What are some of the problems of living in a modern city?
- How do you think cities will change in your country over the next 50 years?

Topic 2      The Environment
- Does your country suffer from pollution problems?
- How does your country's government deal with pollution?
- What do you feel is more important, the environment or people's standard of living? (Why?)
- Do you think overpopulation is an important environment issue?

# PRACTICE TEST 4

# LISTENING

 Download audio recordings for the test here:
https://www.ielts-blog.com/ielts-practice-tests-downloads/

**PART 1**          **Questions 1 – 10**

*Questions 1 – 5*

*Complete Jake's reservation change form below.*

*Write **NO MORE THAN TWO WORDS AND/OR A NUMBER** from the listening for each answer.*

---

**The Sutherland Hotel
Reservation Change Form**

Reservation Number          EZT 486 978

Customer's Name:            Mrs. Jane (**1**) _____

Address:                    (**2**) _____ Richmond Rise
                            Birkdale
                            Auckland

Postcode:                   0626

Date of Birth:              14th (**3**) _____ 1985

Reservation Website Used:   (**4**) _____

(**5**) _____ not charged by the website!

---

## Questions 6 – 10

Complete Jake's summary email confirming the change in hotel reservation.

Write **NO MORE THAN THREE WORDS AND/OR SOME NUMBERS** for each answer.

---

*Re: your reservation change*

Dear Madam,

Thanks for your call. I have made the change you requested to your booking and I have summarised the information below:

The two adults in the booking have not changed. Two children have been added: Mark ((**6**) _____ years) + Max (eight years). The boys will have a twin room with no (**7**) _____. Original booking from Friday 22nd May - Wednesday 27th May. New booking from Saturday 23rd May - Wednesday 27th May.

Price changes: Adult booking 1 day fewer. Boys: Mark is charged the full rate; Max is charged the child rate. Old price NZ$1200; new price NZ$(**8**) _____ exactly.

The booking is held by a VISA card with the last four numbers 8537. Previous (**9**) _____ paid does not need to be increased.

(**10**) _____ is included for all guests in the booking.

Best wishes,
Jake

---

## PART 2          *Questions 11 – 20*

### *Questions 11 and 12*

*Answer the questions below. Write **NO MORE THAN THREE WORDS AND/OR A NUMBER** from the listening for each answer.*

**11**     When was the chocolate factory built?

**12**     How many full-time employees work at the factory?

### *Questions 13 – 15*

*Complete the flow chart describing the tour of the chocolate factory.*
*Write **NO MORE THAN THREE WORDS** from the listening for each answer.*

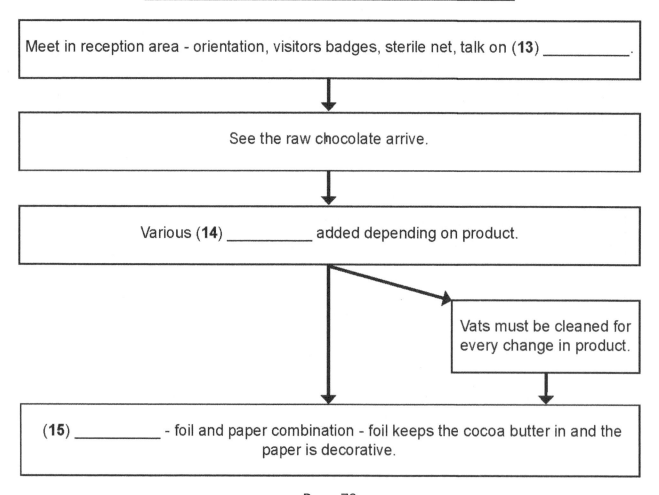

**Chocolate Factory - Tour of Manufacturing Area**

Meet in reception area - orientation, visitors badges, sterile net, talk on **(13)** _____ .

See the raw chocolate arrive.

Various **(14)** _____ added depending on product.

Vats must be cleaned for every change in product.

**(15)** _____ - foil and paper combination - foil keeps the cocoa butter in and the paper is decorative.

## Questions 16 – 20

*Complete the notes below on the second part of the talk on the tour of the chocolate factory. Write* **NO MORE THAN ONE WORD AND/OR A NUMBER** *from the listening for each answer.*

---

Return to admin. area after the manufacturing tour:

> * a film on the history of chocolate
> * a brief (**16**) _____ on the company's marketing + sales strategies

Tasting

The (**17**) _____ will help you choose from all our products; (don't eat too much - especially children)

Administration

*Individuals and Small Groups*

One tour in morning starting at (**18**) _____ a.m.; one tour in afternoon starting at 2 p.m.

> Adults - $13
> Senior citizens - $9
> Children - $6

*Larger and School Tours*

> Adults - $ (**19**) _____
> Senior citizens - $9
> Children - $4 (accompanying school staff free)
> (these tours can be at any time, but must be booked in advance)

* All guides have police screening for working with children
* Free parking for cars and coaches
* Complete (**20**) _____ access
* Guide dogs welcome (but not in the manufacturing areas)

---

## PART 3     *Questions 21 – 30*

### *Questions 21 – 25*

*Complete the tables below on Tina and Edward's course change situations.*

*Write **NO MORE THAN ONE WORD** from the listening for each answer.*

| Tina | | | |
|---|---|---|---|
| | Year 1 Subjects | Main Subject Now | New Main Subject Wanted |
| | History | History | Linguistics |
| | French | | |
| | Linguistics | | |
| Notes | | | |
| Misses linguistics in her 2nd year. Liked history, but finds she has to study too many (**21**) _____ she doesn't want to. Even with 3rd year (**22**) _____, she will still have too many compulsory things to study. | | | |

| Edward | | | |
|---|---|---|---|
| | Year 1 Subjects | Main Subject Now | New Main Subject Wanted |
| | History | History | Earth Sciences |
| | English | | |
| | Earth Sciences | | |
| Notes | | | |
| Studied Earth Sciences in year 1, as he wanted something different; had no problem in the 1st year. Likes History and English, but finds he has too many (**23**) _____ in these subjects. Did additional summer (**24**) _____ and discussed it with his family. In Earth Sciences, students are assessed by smaller assignments, (**25**) _____ and shorter exams. | | | |

## Questions 26 – 28

*Choose **THREE** letters, **A - G**.*

*Which **THREE** people need to sign Edward's form so that he can change subject?*

**A**      Professor Holden

**B**      Doctor Flynn

**C**      Mr Thomas

**D**      Professor Atkins

**E**      Mr Morton

**F**      Miss Morgan

**G**      Professor Evans

## Questions 29 and 30.

*Choose the correct letter **A, B, or C**.*

**29**     Other than taking the forms to the registrar's office, Professor Holden says that the only other way to get the forms to the registrar's office is

    **A**      to give the completed forms to him.

    **B**      to email the completed forms.

    **C**      to post their completed forms.

**30**     The registrar's office is found

    **A**      on the third floor of the offices above the post office.

    **B**      on the third floor of the administrative building opposite the post office.

    **C**      on the second floor of the administrative building opposite the post office.

## PART 4    Questions 31 – 40

### Questions 31 – 34

*Complete the notes and diagram related to the Great Artesian Basin below.*

*Write **NO MORE THAN THREE WORDS** from the listening for each answer.*

---

**The Formation of the Great Artesian Basin**

Gondwana, a land mass created in the Triassic age, had a (**31**) _____ in its north west corner. Due to great movement of the earth over the next 100 million years, the ocean level rose and fell. The natural dip filled with water, which left deposits of (**32**) _____ that created the impermeable stone strata that would hold the Great Artesian Basin's water reservoir.

---

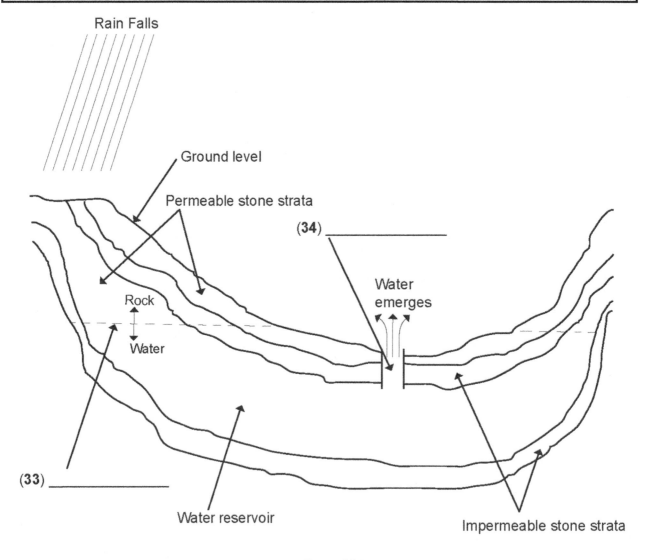

---

## Questions 35 – 40

*Complete the notes below. Write **NO MORE THAN THREE WORDS** from the listening for each answer.*

* It's estimated 65,000,000,000 megalitres are in the Great Artesian Basin.
* It brings life to arid areas in Australia - various flora and fauna survive in these unique (**35**) _____.
* Water also gets into river systems helping them flow in dry times.
* Man-made bore holes create artesian wells - these support agriculture and (**36**) _____.

* Modern usage of the Great Artesian Basin has caused problems:
    Some wells and sources are dry.
    Some bore holes can't be turned off - wastes water and supports weeds + feral animals.
    95% of water from these running bore holes (**37**) _____ or soaks away.
    Many old bore holes badly made - water escapes.

* New strategy created to manage the water:
    Capping - putting lids on bores (water accessed by using a (**38**) _____).
    Piping - replaces channels / drains; water goes to (**39**) _____ preventing wastage.

* Strategy to protect water from the Great Artesian Basin is vital to all of Australia. If water from the Great Artesian Basin is lost...
    ... 70 towns would disappear.
    ... AUS$1 billion would be lost from the beef, wool and sheep industries.
    ... the effect on Australia's food production system would mean that more food would have to be imported (this would affect Australia's (**40**) _____ and whole economy).

# READING

## READING PASSAGE 1

*You should spend about 20 minutes on **Questions 1 - 13**, which are based on Reading Passage 1 below.*

### Bricks - The Versatile Building Material

Bricks are one of the oldest known building materials dating back to 7000 BCE. The oldest found were sun-dried mud bricks in southern Turkey and these would have been standard in those days. Although sun-dried mud bricks worked reasonably well, especially in moderate climates, fired bricks were found to be more resistant to harsher weather conditions and so fired bricks are much more reliable for use in permanent buildings. Fired brick are also useful in hotter climates, as they can absorb any heat generated throughout the day and then release it at night.

The Romans also distinguished between the bricks they used that were dried by the sun and air and the bricks that were fired in a kiln. The Romans were real brick connoisseurs. They preferred to make their bricks in the spring and hold on to their bricks for two years, before they were used or sold. They only used clay that was whitish or red for their bricks. The Romans passed on their skills around their sphere of influence and were especially successful at using their mobile kilns to introduce kiln-fired bricks to the whole of the Roman Empire.

During the twelfth century, bricks were introduced to northern Germany from northern Italy. This created the 'brick Gothic period,' which was a reduced style of Gothic architecture previously very common in northern Europe. The buildings around this time were mainly built from fired red clay bricks. The brick Gothic period can be categorised by the lack of figural architectural sculptures that had previously been carved in stone, as the Gothic figures were impossible to create out of bulky bricks at that time.

Bricks suffered a setback during the Renaissance and Baroque periods, with exposed brick walls becoming unpopular and brickwork being generally covered by plaster. Only during the mid eighteenth century did visible brick walls again regain some popularity.

Bricks today are more commonly used in the construction of buildings than any other material, except wood. Brick architecture is dominant within its field and a great industry has developed and invested in the manufacture of many different types of bricks of all shapes and colours. With modern machinery, earth moving equipment, powerful electric motors and modern tunnel kilns, making bricks has become much more productive and efficient. Bricks can be made from a variety of materials, the most common being clay, but they can also be made of calcium silicate and concrete.

Good quality bricks have major advantages over stone as they are reliable, weather resistant and can tolerate acids, pollution and fire. They are also much cheaper than cut stonework. Bricks can be made to any specification in colour, size and shape, which makes them easier to build with than stone. On the other hand, there are some bricks that are more porous and therefore more susceptible to damage from dampness when exposed to water. For best results in any construction work, the correct brick must be chosen in accordance with the job specifications.

Today, bricks are mainly manufactured in factories, usually employing one of three principal methods - the soft mud process, the stiff mud process and the dry clay process. In the past, bricks were largely manufactured by hand, and there are still artisanal companies that specialise in this product. The process involves putting the clay, water and additives into a large pit, where it is all mixed together by a tempering wheel, often still moved by horse power. Once the mixture is of the correct consistency, the clay is removed and pressed into moulds by hand. To prevent the brick from sticking to the mould, the brick is coated in either sand or water, though coating a brick with sand gives an overall better finish to it. Once shaped, the bricks are laid outside to dry by air and sun for three to four days. If these bricks left outside for the drying process are exposed to a shower, the water can leave indentations on the brick, which, although not affecting the strength of the brick, is considered very undesirable. After drying, the bricks are then transferred to the kiln for firing and this creates the finished product. Bricks are now more generally made by manufacturing processes using machinery. This is a large-scale effort and produces bricks that have been fired in patent kilns.

Today's bricks are also specially designed to be efficient at insulation. If their composition is correct and their laying accurate, a good brick wall around a house can save the occupants a significant amount of money. This is primarily achieved today through cavity wall insulation. Insulating bricks are built in two separate leaves, as they are called in the trade. The gap between the inner and outer leaves of brickwork depends on the type of insulation used, but there should be enough space for a gap of twenty millimetres between the insulating material in the cavity and the two leaves on either side. The air in these gaps is an efficient insulator by itself. Cavity walls have also replaced solid walls, because they are more resistant to rain penetration. Because two leaves are necessary, a strong brick manufacturing industry is essential, so that enough good quality insulating bricks are plentifully available.

**Questions 1 – 5**

*Do the following statements agree with the information given in the text?*

*In boxes 1 – 5 on your answer sheet write:*

| | |
|---|---|
| **TRUE** | *if the statement agrees with the information* |
| **FALSE** | *if the statement contradicts the information* |
| **NOT GIVEN** | *if there is no information on this* |

1    Fired bricks are not efficient in countries with hot weather, as they absorb too much heat.

2    Roman brick production was determined by which season it was.

3    The bricks that led to the brick Gothic period in northern Germany were popular with house builders.

4    Buildings showing brickwork were generally not liked during the Renaissance.

5    Some types of bricks can soak up too much water due to their absorbent qualities.

**Questions 6 – 11**

*Complete the flow chart below.*

*Write **NO MORE THAN TWO WORDS** from the text for each answer.*

*Write your answers in boxes **6 – 11** on your answer sheet.*

### Making Hand-made Bricks

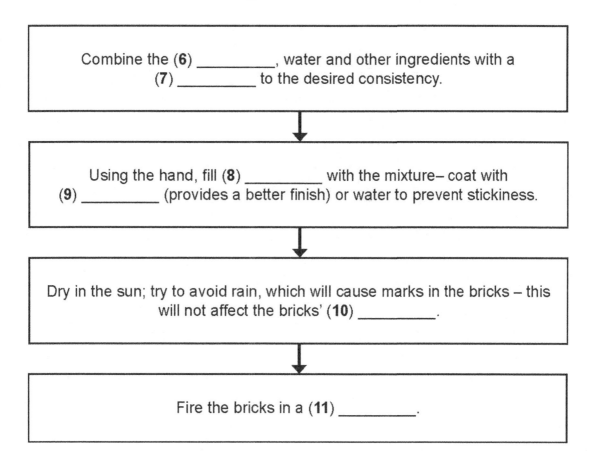

Combine the (**6**) _____, water and other ingredients with a (**7**) _____ to the desired consistency.

⬇

Using the hand, fill (**8**) _____ with the mixture– coat with (**9**) _____ (provides a better finish) or water to prevent stickiness.

⬇

Dry in the sun; try to avoid rain, which will cause marks in the bricks – this will not affect the bricks' (**10**) _____.

⬇

Fire the bricks in a (**11**) _____.

## Questions 12 and 13

*Label the diagram below.*

*Write* **NO MORE THAN TWO WORDS AND/OR A NUMBER** *from the text for each answer.*

*Write your answers in boxes* **12 and 13** *on your answer sheet.*

**Cavity Wall Insulation**

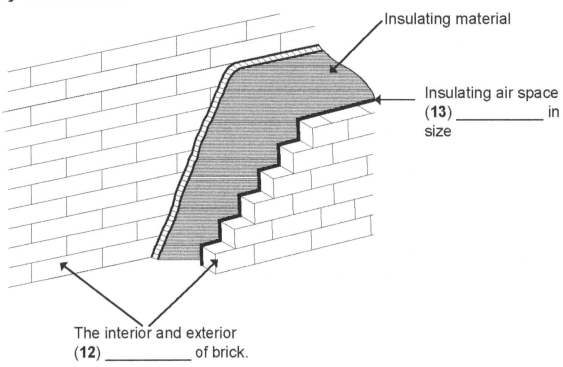

Insulating material

Insulating air space
(**13**) _____ in size

The interior and exterior
(**12**) _____ of brick.

## READING PASSAGE 2

You should spend about 20 minutes on **Questions 14 - 26**, which are based on Reading Passage 2 below.

### The Rise of Agritourism

In advanced industrialised countries, small farmers have been challenged by changing economic and social conditions, such as increased global competition, falling commodity prices, and capital- and technology-intensive agricultural production. In addition, there has been added public pressure to make expensive changes in farming methods, due to public environmental concerns about industrialised agricultural production in combination with political pressures to reduce agricultural subsidies. These changing economic and social conditions have disproportionately impacted smaller farms in Europe and the US.

Agritourism is becoming an increasingly popular way for rural property owners to earn additional income from agricultural properties. In addition to more traditional farm tours and seasonal activities, such as hay rides, corn mazes and u-pick fruits, farm owners are devising new ways to bring people to their door by offering more entertainment-oriented activities. Some farmers are offering their barns as venues for weddings, parties, dances and other special events. Others are opening their homes to visitors for vacations, so guests can experience life on a working farm by helping out with routine farm chores, such as feeding or herding the livestock, milking the animals, making cheese, collecting eggs, picking vegetables and preparing farm fresh meals. Agritourism works in combination with a growing public desire to engage in rural experiences and outdoor recreational activities. By combining agriculture and tourism, agritourism offers these rural experiences to urban residents and economic diversification to farmers.

Part of the attraction of agritourism is the nostalgia it creates for a simpler time and its authenticity. Tourists are being sold, not only on beautiful sceneries and visual aesthetics, but also experiences that are meant to open up a new world for these customers who are tired of the hustle and bustle of city life. Authenticity has been an abiding theme in tourism studies and it may have a special meaning in this combination of agriculture and tourism. For one thing, the image of the family farm remains imbued with deep authenticity, the surviving representation of an old world ideal. To partake in agritourism is therefore likely to convey the sense of having a deeply authentic experience. Critics have claimed that this desire to reconnect with the life world of one's ancestors may conflict with the nature of modern agriculture and whether the tourist will want to face its true realities. It seems therefore that often the most distinctive innovative effort involves the reinvention of tradition and rural tourism products. Examples are the recreation of home-produced products long since replaced by manufactured commodities and the provision of hands-on-experiences in crafts often recreated for tourists. As a result, some critics argue that the tourists who are running to the countryside are over-crowding and ruining the pristine beauty that they so desperately want to experience.

Agritourism can benefit the life and economy of local communities, as well as the farms themselves. Agritourism firstly means that some farms can continue in business and employ workers. Employment underscores the genuine importance of agritourism farms to local economies, as rural communities are usually areas that both have high unemployment and few alternatives for the unemployed to find work. Secondly, a significant number of agritourists come from areas reasonably local to the visited farms. This means that tourist spending on agritourism often stays in the region, helping to generate taxable revenues and more disposable incomes. The U.S. Department of Agriculture's agricultural census, taken every five years, found that last year approximately 23,000 farms took part in agritourism. These farms each earned $24,300 from agritourism, compared to five years ago, when farms engaged in this brought in only $7,200 per farm. The trend is clearly growing and the money generated will stimulate local economies. Thirdly, agritourism benefits the local community in terms of education. Many farms offer tours for elementary school-age children, who can learn where their food is coming from and how it is produced.

Farms choosing to develop agritourism have had reasonable government support. Over the last 20 years, European Union countries have spent 2 billion euros to subsidise agritourism development in rural farming areas that cannot compete in a global market with declining commodity prices. This, in turn, helps governments by keeping farmers on land, protecting picturesque rural landscapes that attract tourists, and supporting the production of agricultural products from the region. As well as finance, local and national governments should create in the areas under their jurisdiction favourable environments for the development of agritourism, by changing regulatory and tax constraints, so that more farms are encouraged to enter the industry.

It is clear that there are strong economic and social benefits that agritourism can provide farmers, customers and the local areas where the farms are situated. Agritourism contributes to and enhances the quality of life in communities by expanding recreational opportunities, differentiating rural economies, and promoting the retention of agricultural lands. Working agricultural landscapes reflect the efforts of generations of farm families and often provide a defining sense of culture, heritage, and rural character. Agritourism provides educational opportunities for school children and adults to learn about this agrarian heritage, the production of food, and resource stewardship. Finally, many agritourism operations provide consumers with direct access to fresh farm goods. Agritourism is an industry with an enormous potential for growth. With it, farming could become more efficient and sustainable, rural areas could become more beautiful and farmers could become better off and more significant employers and contributors to economies.

**Questions 14 – 19**

*Choose the correct letter **A, B, C or D**.*

*Write the correct letter in boxes **14 - 19** on your answer sheet.*

**14**    Farmers today face demands from the public about

    **A**    reacting to global competition.
    **B**    improving workers' conditions.
    **C**    changing to more environmentally friendly production methods.
    **D**    making production cheaper.

**15**    Farmers today are experiencing pressure from governments, as the latter wishes to

    **A**    reduce the amount of money they provide to help farmers.
    **B**    increase taxes to gain more public income.
    **C**    force farmers to employ more workers.
    **D**    reduce the amount of pesticides used in agricultural production.

**16**    Farmers can attract tourists by

    **A**    undercutting the competition of traditional holidays on prices.
    **B**    being close to transport hubs.
    **C**    letting people get married on the farm.
    **D**    marketing on a door-by-door basis.

**17**    Farming authenticity partly depends on

    **A**    the beauty of the farms' surroundings.
    **B**    the public's traditional perceptions of a small farm.
    **C**    how the farm workers dress and behave.
    **D**    the type of livestock the farms have.

**18**    Farms can create authenticity by

    **A**    making tourist workers get up very early in the morning.
    **B**    having interactive displays of farm workings.
    **C**    not showing animals being killed.
    **D**    re-establishing old processes that are not usually used any more.

**19**    One criticism of agritourism is that
    **A**    farm workers lose their jobs.
    **B**    tourists change how farms operate.
    **C**    the extra numbers of people in the countryside spoil its appeal.
    **D**    only the farmer receives the extra income.

**Questions 20 – 26**

*Complete the notes below.*

Write **NO MORE THAN THREE WORDS** *for each answer.*

*Write your answers in boxes* **20 - 26** *on your answer sheet.*

---

### The Benefits of Agritourism

* Farms continue in business and are employers.

* Tourist (**20**) _____ remains in the area.

* It generates taxes and creates increased numbers of (**21**) _____.

* Local economies grow because of the extra money spent.

* Children can learn about farming.

* (**22**) _____ benefit by keeping farms in operation on the land.

* Rural (**23**) _____ are preserved.

* Farming goods of the (**24**) _____ continue to be manufactured.

* Improved quality of life and more recreational possibilities in communities.

* Diversified (**25**) _____.

* Land remains in use by agriculture.

* Education for all.

* People can easily buy (**26**) _____.

---

## READING PASSAGE 3

*You should spend about 20 minutes on **Questions 27 - 40**, which are based on Reading Passage 3 below.*

### The Fight Against Polio

**Paragraph A**

The poliovirus is one of the smallest and simplest viruses. It is usually spread by just dirty fingers and in most cases is confined to the gut. As the virus travels down the intestine, it induces the body to produce antibodies against it, which will protect the person against future attacks. In about one per cent of cases, the virus floods into the bloodstream and infects the nerve cells in the spinal cord that drive the muscles. This causes the characteristic paralysis, which can affect one or more limbs and/or the muscles of respiration, in which case artificial ventilation, for example with the iron lung, may be needed to keep the patient breathing and alive. The iron lung, which was officially known as a negative pressure ventilator, was invented hundreds of years ago, but was further developed in the 1930's to help with the world polio outbreaks. At one point, the need for iron lungs was so high that they were used with a patient within an hour of their manufacture.

**Paragraph B**

Polio originally caused sporadic clusters of paralysis, especially in children. For some reason, this pattern changed during the late nineteenth century into explosive epidemics, which swept through many countries each summer. The first major outbreak, on the East Coast of the USA in the summer of 1916, caused 25,000 cases of paralysis and 6,000 deaths. Draconian public health measures were powerless to prevent the spread of the disease, resulting in widespread panic across America. Each year, panic resurfaced as the polio season approached, with the wealthy leaving towns and cities in droves.

**Paragraph C**

This fear of polio was deliberately fuelled and exploited by the March of Dimes, an American fund-raising organisation set up by President Franklin D Roosevelt, himself a polio survivor. The March of Dimes raised vast sums, and funded both practical support for polio victims and their families, and the research programmes that ultimately resulted in effective polio vaccines.

**Paragraph D**

Polio can be prevented but not cured. Treatments proposed for patients with acute polio have included barbaric measures, such as branding the child's back with a red-hot poker and 'brain washout therapy'. Less dramatic were massive doses of vitamin C and chemically modified cobra venom. None of these had any impact on paralysis or survival, and some were positively dangerous. The iron lung could rescue patients from suffocation if their respiratory muscles were paralysed, but the iron lung itself carried considerable risks. Until chest infections could be properly treated, seventy per cent of patients put inside the iron lung died there.

**Paragraph E**

Two rival strategies were used to develop vaccines to protect against polio. Jonas Salk (1914–1998) favoured an 'inactivated polio vaccine' (IPV), in which wild polioviruses are 'killed' with formalin, so that they can no longer replicate and spread into the spinal cord. IPV is injected into a muscle and causes protective antibodies to appear in the bloodstream. The 'oral polio vaccine' (OPV) developed by Albert Sabin (1906–1993) relies on the fact that polioviruses forced to grow under unfavourable conditions in the laboratory will undergo mutation into forms that can no longer invade the spinal cord. The OPV virus is still 'alive' and able to replicate, but cannot enter the spinal cord and cause paralysis. OPV is taken by mouth and, like a wild poliovirus, induces immunity against itself in the gut wall as it travels through the intestine. It therefore provides a different type of immunity protection when compared with the Salk vaccine.

**Paragraph F**

Salk's IPV was the first polio vaccine to be tested on a large scale, in massive clinical trials in 1954 involving 1.8 million American children. Following the sensational declaration that his vaccine 'works and is safe', Salk became a national and international hero, and mass vaccination of children with his IPV began immediately. Vaccination continued despite a tragic outbreak of paralytic (and sometimes fatal) polio due to contamination of the Salk vaccine with wild poliovirus, which was the result of carelessness in the vaccine production plant. Numbers of paralytic cases and deaths from polio fell dramatically in the USA over the next few years, and Salk's vaccine was taken up across the world. Sabin's OPV, being cheaper, more effective and easier to give, later superseded the Salk vaccine. Given correctly, both vaccines protect against polio and are overwhelmingly safe. There is an exceedingly low risk (one in 500,000 vaccinations) of Sabin's OPV reverting to a paralysing variant, a drawback that Sabin always refused to acknowledge.

**Paragraph G**

Polio vaccine not only protects individuals, but, if given intensively and on a massive scale, can prevent the virus from spreading and so stamp it out. In 1988, various organisations set out to clear the planet of polio through a worldwide vaccination campaign. The hope was that polio would follow the example of smallpox, which was exterminated by intensive global vaccination during the late 1970's. Now, after 26 years, polio is tantalisingly close to being eradicated, with just 200 paralytic cases worldwide last year, as compared with over 300,000 in 1988. Tragically, though, endemic polio continues to cling on in three areas, Afghanistan, Pakistan and Northern Nigeria, largely because of anti-western ideology that is backed up by intimidation, death threats and the murder of many vaccinators and their supporters. Usually refugees, but also other travellers, have reintroduced polio to other countries, for example Syria, Lebanon and various African states, which had been previously cleared of polio. Unfortunately, it is now very unlikely that polio will be eradicated within the next two to three years and it seems that the final extermination of the virus will depend as much on diplomacy as on medicine and science.

Glossary

Draconian – severe or harsh.

In droves – in large numbers.

*Questions 27 – 33*

*The text on the previous pages has 7 paragraphs **A - G**.*

*Which paragraph contains the following information?*

*Write your answers in boxes **27 – 33** on your answer sheet.*

27      The OPV protects people in the same way as a wild virus works in the body.

28      Panic was intentionally created in order to raise money to fight polio.

29      The OPV was more successful than the IPV at preventing polio.

30      The US polio outbreaks caused some people to move away from high population areas in the summers.

31      Extremism is one barrier to the eradication of polio.

32      Iron lungs were in great demand because the numbers of people sick with polio.

33      One medicine used to treat polio was based on snake poison.

**Questions 34 – 37**

*Complete the summary below.*

*Write **NO MORE THAN ONE WORD** from the text for each answer.*

*Write your answers in boxes **34 - 37** on your answer sheet.*

---

**THE TWO POLIO VACCINES**

Salk developed one of the two anti-polio vaccines by using (**34**) _____ to stop the ability of the polio virus to attack the spinal cord. The vaccine's presence after injection therefore causes the creation of antibodies. Sabin's other vaccine uses induced (**35**) _____ to stop the ability of the virus to attack the spinal cord. After administration, it too creates antibodies.

After large-scale (**36**) _____, the IPV was declared safe and was used for vaccination in the US. Salk was a hero, despite one outbreak of polio due to a contaminated vaccine. The cheaper OPV became more popular over time. Both vaccines are effective, though there is a possible and unlikely danger of an unsafe (**37**) _____ developing in the IPV.

---

**Questions 38 – 40**

*Answer the questions below.*

*Write **NO MORE THAN THREE WORDS AND/OR A NUMBER** from the text for each answer.*
*Write your answers in boxes **38 - 40** on your answer sheet.*

**38**     What group is especially prone to the paralysis caused by polio?

**39**     What proportion of people did not survive treatment in the iron lung without effective chest treatment?

**40**     Who have been the most significant cause for the reintroduction of polio into countries where it was previous eradicated?

# WRITING

## WRITING TASK 1

*You should spend about 20 minutes on this task.*

**The bar chart below shows the average Australian water consumption in selected cities for last year. The pie chart shows the distribution of Australian water consumption for last year.**

**Summarise the information by selecting and reporting the main features, and make comparisons where relevant.**

*You should write at least 150 words.*

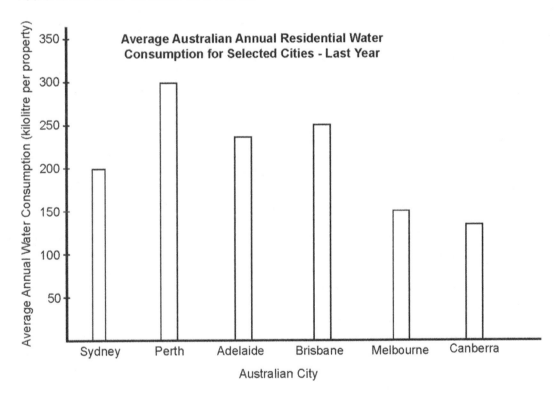

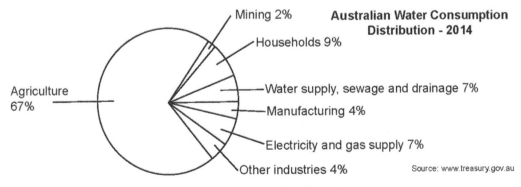

## WRITING TASK 2

*You should spend about 40 minutes on this task.*

*Write about the following topic:*

> **The breakthroughs in medical science are by far the most significant advances in world society over the last two centuries.**
>
> **Discuss this statement and give your opinion.**

*Give reasons for your answer and include any relevant examples from your knowledge or experience.*

*You should write at least 250 words.*

# SPEAKING

## PART 1

- Can you describe one of the rooms in your house/flat?
- Do you prefer living in a big house/flat or a small one? (Why?)
- What are some of the disadvantages of living in a big house?

Topic 1         Entertainment
- What is the most popular form of entertainment in your country?
- Do people in your country usually prefer to go out or stay at home in the evenings?
- Why do you think that successful entertainers are often paid so much?
- How popular is watching sport in your country as a form of entertainment?

Topic 2         Teenagers
- What is life like for a teenager in your country?
- What are some of the challenges that teenagers face today?
- Do you think teenagers should be allowed to drive? (Why/Why not?)
- What are parents' attitudes to boyfriends and girlfriends for teenagers in your country?

## PART 2

Describe something you have bought recently
You should say:
        what it is
        where you bought it
        what it looks like
and explain why you needed to buy this thing.

## PART 3

Topic 1         Luxury
- What luxury item would you choose if you could have any one thing?
- Do you think luxury possessions bring happiness? (Why/Why not?)
- Should luxury items be taxed at a higher rate? (Why/Why not?)
- How have the lives of rich people changed over the last 30 years?

Topic 2         The Food Supply
- Where is your country's food mainly produced?
- What are some of the challenges that face food producers today?
- Do you believe that the world should use genetically modified food? (Why/Why not?)
- How can we reduce the amount of food wasted today both domestically and commercially?

# PRACTICE TEST 5

## LISTENING

 Download audio recordings for the test here:
https://www.ielts-blog.com/ielts-practice-tests-downloads/

### PART 1          *Questions 1 – 10*

**Questions 1 – 5**

*Complete Roger's customer form below.*

*Write **NO MORE THAN THREE WORDS AND/OR A NUMBER** from the listening for each answer.*

---

**Southern Trains
Special Ticket Form**

| | |
|---|---|
| Type of Ticket: | Season |
| Customer's Name: | Sandra (**1**) _____ |
| Address: | (**2**) _____ Andover Way<br>Stanton<br>ST6 3ED |
| Date of Birth: | 8th October (**3**) _____ |
| Previous Ticket: | YES / (NO) |
| Email Address: | sandra@(**4**) _____.com |
| Telephone:  Home: | n/a |
| Work: | n/a |
| Cell: | 05 (**5**) _____ 495 712 |

---

## Questions 6 – 10

*Circle the correct letters* **A - C**.

**6**     For what journey will Sandra use her season ticket?

     **A**     Stanton to Bexington
     **B**     Stanton to Petersfield
     **C**     Stanton to Amberton

**7**     What type of ticket options does Sandra choose?

     **A**     Off-peak with weekends
     **B**     Peak with weekends
     **C**     Peak without weekends

**8**     What class of season ticket does Sandra choose?

     **A**     First class
     **B**     Second class
     **C**     Variable class

**9**     What is the monthly price of Sandra's season ticket?

     **A**     $98
     **B**     $158.40
     **C**     $172

**10**     From which platform will Sandra's trains leave?

     **A**     4
     **B**     7
     **C**     6

## PART 2     *Questions 11 - 20*

### Questions 11 – 15

*Match the correct level at the Paradise Hotel with the needs given in questions* **11 - 15**.

Level 1       Level 2       Level 3       Level 4
Level 5       Level 6       Level 7

**11**     A guest wants to see the concierge.

**12**     A guest wants to go to room 412.

**13**     A guest wants to go to the beach.

**14**     A guest wants to eat at the seafood restaurant.

**15**     A guest wants to do a yoga class.

### Questions 16 – 20

*Answer the questions below. Write* **NO MORE THAN THREE WORDS AND/OR A NUMBER** *from the listening for each answer.*

**16**     When will Monday's entertainment evening end?

**17**     Where will the quiz be held?

**18**     Who will sing the first song at the karaoke night?

**19**     Where can people book a table for the jazz night?

**20**     Where will live music be playing on Saturday and Sunday evenings?

## PART 3    Questions 21 – 30

### Questions 21 and 22

Complete the table below on the advantages and disadvantages of the cigarette factory site.

Write **NO MORE THAN TWO WORDS** from the listening for each answer.

| Location | Advantages | Disadvantages |
|---|---|---|
| Cigarette factory in town centre | Convenient<br>Possible grants from the (**21**) _____ | No room for a (**22**) _____<br>High site cost |

### Questions 23 – 25

Complete the sentences below.

Write **NO MORE THAN TWO WORDS** from the listening for each answer.

**23**    The financial part of the students' project includes detailing start-up costs and ten years of _____ of revenue.

**24**    Tony points out that lots of construction work for _____ would be required to shelter the field survey site from flooding.

**25**    Because there is always a lot of people travelling to the airport, there is lots of _____ already in place.

**Questions 26 – 29**

*Who will do each of the following jobs?*

| | |
|---|---|
| **A** | Alison |
| **B** | Tony |
| **C** | Sophie |
| **D** | Greg |

*Write the correct letter, **A, B, C or D** on your answer sheet.*

26    Obtain permission to be on the land they want to survey

27    Search for other development plans on the land they want to survey

28    Text the postcode of the land they want to survey

29    Check that the equipment is free

**Question 30**

*Choose the correct letter **A, B, or C**.*

30    How did Tony get the money with which he will pay the deposit?

**A**    A bank loan

**B**    Some work he did

**C**    Borrowed it from his parents

## PART 4     Questions 31 – 40

### Questions 31 – 34

Complete the table below on events related to tea mentioned in the listening.

Write **NO MORE THAN TWO WORDS** from the listening for each answer.

| Time Frame | Events |
|---|---|
| 200 B.C. | First records of tea drunk in (**31**) _____ |
| Latter ½ of the 16th century | Tea mentioned as a drink for Europeans |
| Last years of the 16th century | Dutch import tea to Europe commercially as they take over Portuguese (**32**) _____ |
| The seventeenth century | British adopted tea |
| 1689 | First (**33**) _____ on tea in leaf form |
| The eighteenth century | Debate over whether tea is healthy or not |
| The mid - nineteenth century | Temperance movement recommended tea as an alternative to (**34**) _____ |
| 1964 | Tax on tea is abolished |

### Questions 35 – 37

Label the pie chart below on world tea consumption. Write **NO MORE THAN THREE WORDS AND/OR A NUMBER** from the listening for each answer.

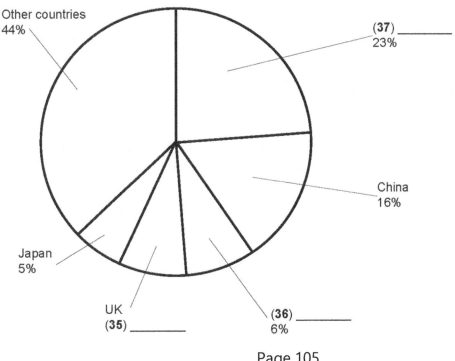

Other countries
44%

(37) _____
23%

China
16%

Japan
5%

UK
(35) _____

(36) _____
6%

## Questions 38 – 40

*Complete the flow chart describing the process for making tea below. Write **NO MORE THAN ONE WORD AND/OR A NUMBER** from the listening for each answer.*

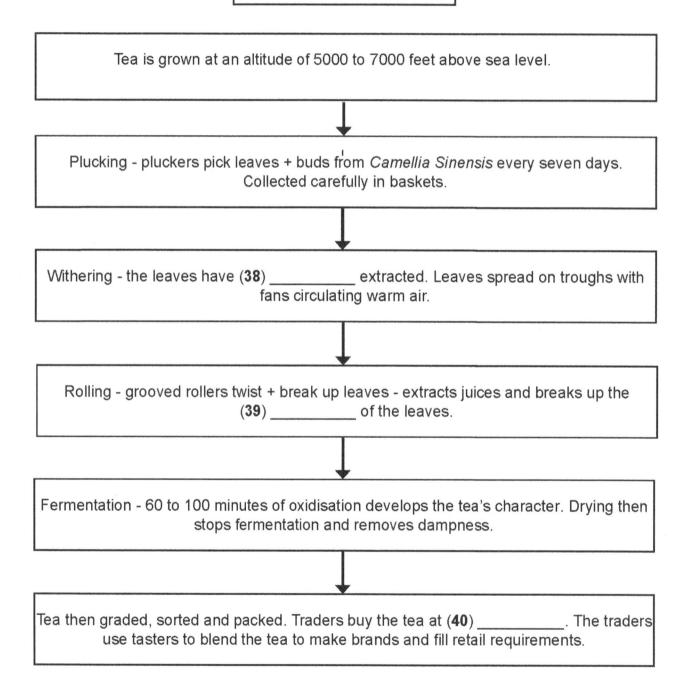

**The Process for Making Tea**

Tea is grown at an altitude of 5000 to 7000 feet above sea level.

⬇

Plucking - pluckers pick leaves + buds from *Camellia Sinensis* every seven days. Collected carefully in baskets.

⬇

Withering - the leaves have (**38**) _____ extracted. Leaves spread on troughs with fans circulating warm air.

⬇

Rolling - grooved rollers twist + break up leaves - extracts juices and breaks up the (**39**) _____ of the leaves.

⬇

Fermentation - 60 to 100 minutes of oxidisation develops the tea's character. Drying then stops fermentation and removes dampness.

⬇

Tea then graded, sorted and packed. Traders buy the tea at (**40**) _____. The traders use tasters to blend the tea to make brands and fill retail requirements.

# READING

## READING PASSAGE 1

*You should spend about 20 minutes on **Questions 1 - 13**, which are based on Reading Passage 1 below.*

### Sleep

Historically, it was difficult to study sleep. Not much can be gleaned from observing recumbent persons and questionnaires are no use, because people remember little of their experience during sleep. The breakthrough came in the 1950's with electroencephalogram (EEG) recordings of brain electrical activity, when it was confirmed that sleep is anything but dormant.

We need sleep for biological restoration. It promotes cell growth, regeneration and memory consolidation. By shutting down most of the body's machinery, resources can be focused on repairing damage and development. When people are deprived of sleep for any reason, there is deterioration in performance, particularly on tasks requiring concentration, and eventually, behaviour becomes shambolic. The individual becomes progressively incoherent and irritable and, after a few days, may experience delusions and hallucinations. The disruptive effects of sleep deprivation have even been successfully used as a basis of persuasion in interrogation.

A vital part of sleep is dreaming, which happens most intensively during rapid eye movement (REM) sleep. We typically spend more than two hours each night dreaming, though this is often spread over four or five separate periods. Infants spend up to 50 per cent of their sleep time in REM sleep, which is understandable when one realises that REM sleep is the time used for brain development, as well as learning, thinking, and organising information. If people are woken when REM sleep commences, depriving them specifically of dream-sleep, the proportion of REM sleep increases once they fall asleep again to make up what was lost. This suggests that REM sleep is an essential aspect of sleep.

Sleep and sleep-related problems play a role in a large number of human disorders and affect almost every field of medicine. For example, problems like a stroke tend to occur more frequently during the night and early morning, due to changes in hormones, heart rate, and other characteristics associated with sleep. Sleep also affects some kinds of epilepsy in complex ways. REM sleep seems to help prevent seizures that begin in one part of the brain from spreading to other brain regions, while deep sleep may promote the spread of these seizures. Sleep deprivation can also trigger seizures in people with some types of epilepsy.

The neurons that control sleep interact strongly with the immune system. As anyone who has had the flu knows, infectious diseases tend to make people feel sleepy. This probably happens because cytokines, chemicals produced while fighting an infection, are powerful sleep-inducing substances. Sleep helps the body conserve energy that the body's immune system needs to mount an attack.

Sleeping problems occur in almost all people with mental disorders, including those with depression and schizophrenia. People with depression, for example, often awaken in the early hours of the morning and find themselves unable to get back to sleep. The amount of sleep a person gets also strongly influences the symptoms of mental disorders. Sleep deprivation is an effective therapy for people with certain types of depression, while it can actually cause depression in other people. Extreme sleep deprivation can lead to a seemingly psychotic state of paranoia and hallucinations in otherwise healthy people, and disrupted sleep can trigger episodes of mania in people with manic depression.

Sleeping problems are common in many other disorders as well, including Alzheimer's disease, stroke, cancer, and head injury. These sleeping problems may arise from changes in the brain regions and neurotransmitters that control sleep, or from the drugs used to control symptoms of other disorders. In patients who are hospitalised or who receive round-the-clock care, treatment schedules or hospital routines also may disrupt sleep. The old joke about a patient being awakened by a nurse so he could take a sleeping pill contains a grain of truth. Once sleeping problems develop, they can add to a person's impairment and cause confusion, frustration, or depression. Patients who are unable to sleep also notice pain more and may increase their requests for pain medication. Better management of sleeping problems in people who have a variety of disorders could improve the health of these patients and their quality of life.

Insomnia is a widespread affliction. It is linked with conditions such as depression and chronic pain, but occurs also in otherwise healthy people. It is often due to temporary life circumstances, like trouble at work or anticipation of an exciting event, however, some people just have difficulty sleeping regardless of circumstances. What is interesting is that complaints of sleeplessness are often exaggerated, because people remember more easily the times they are awake during the night than the times they are asleep. When insomniacs are observed in a sleep lab, their EEG records often suggest that their sleep pattern is fairly normal, even though in the morning they maintain they hardly slept a wink. Various devices for monitoring one's own sleep patterns are now marketed, for example mobile phone apps connected with forehead electrodes.

The fact that a third of our life is spent in sleep would, in itself, be sufficient justification for studying it scientifically. The discovery that it is not just a passive state, but a highly active process of profound biological and psychological importance, has led to great efforts in recent decades to further our understanding of it. Despite that, we are far from unravelling all of sleep's mysteries.

**Questions 1 – 7**

Complete the notes below.

Write **NO MORE THAN TWO WORDS** for each answer.

Write your answers in boxes **1 - 7** on your answer sheet.

---

### Sleep

* Sleep study only advanced after the electroencephalogram started to be used.

* Sleep is used to restore the body and cells, and strengthen the (**1**) _____.

* With little sleep, people operate worse, especially when (**2**) _____ is needed.

* The effects of sleep deprivation can be severe and have been used in interrogations.

* REM sleep is when dreaming occurs; important especially for (**3**) _____, who need a lot of REM sleep for their brains.

* If REM sleep is lost, the body increases the (**4**) _____ of REM sleep in the next sleep to make it up.

* Strokes are more common during or after sleep, and (**5**) _____ and other seizures can both be caused and prevented by sleep.

* Sleep is closely associated with the (**6**) _____, as cytokines produced while the body fights infectious disease induce sleepiness; sleeping when sick helps people save the (**7**) _____ to fight infections.

---

**Questions 8 – 13**

*Do the following statements agree with the information given in the text?*

*In boxes **8 – 13** on your answer sheet write:*

> **TRUE**          *if the statement agrees with the information*
> **FALSE**         *if the statement contradicts the information*
> **NOT GIVEN**     *if there is no information on this*

8    A lack of sleep can both help and hinder people suffering from depression.

9    Better sleep routines can help people who suffer from Parkinson's disease.

10   People who are sleep-deprived actually have a better tolerance to pain.

11   In spite of media reports, insomnia is not a common problem.

12   Insomniacs often sleep more than they realise.

13   Overuse of mobile phone apps can cause insomnia in some people.

## READING PASSAGE 2

*You should spend about 20 minutes on **Questions 14 - 26**, which are based on Reading Passage 2 below.*

### Comets

Comets arrive to grace our skies every year; some are new to the inner Solar System, and some are old friends on a repeat visit, but only comparatively rarely do they reach sufficient brightness to become apparent to the unaided eye.

Comets do not behave like any other object that we can observe in the night sky with the unaided eye. Stars remain fixed in the pattern of their constellations, and are regular in their motion through the sky from one night to the next, and from one month to the next. A planet follows a fairly slow but expected path. By comparison, a comet is a totally different kind of event: it will appear unexpectedly and at any place in the sky, it will change position from one night to the next relative to the background of stars, and its path will be along a separate direction and path across the sky from the planets and stars. During the few weeks or months that it is observable, it will first steadily increase in brightness from one night to the next, may change its shape – growing bigger, longer or extra tails – and then wane to invisibility, never to be seen again. Throughout history, comets have always signified evil, war and death, and they were supposed to leave chaos and calamity in their wake. Indeed, plenty of past comets have been blamed by the astrologers of their day for bringing or marking misfortune.

There have been many spectacular comets throughout history; on average we are visited by what is termed a 'great comet' about three times a century. This appellation is saved for those comets that reach exceptional brightness. The most famous of all comets is Halley's comet; not that it is the most spectacular, but study of its orbit by the English astronomer, Edmond Halley, was fundamental to pinning down the real nature of comets. During the 17th century, Halley was using Newton's new mathematics of calculus to try to characterise the orbits of twenty-four comets from sightings recorded over the previous four centuries. He realised that the orbital path of the bright comet recently seen in 1682 was very similar to that followed by two other comets – one observed in 1531 and one in 1607. All moved in a retrograde direction (i.e. opposite to the revolution of the planets round the Sun), following an elliptical orbit that had a similar orientation to the plane of the planets' motion. The great comet of 1456 was also known to have travelled in a retrograde direction. Halley's inspiration was to realise that these were four apparitions of the same comet, following a set path around the Sun, but which only became apparent to observers on Earth when its orbit returned the comet to the inner Solar System, after an interval of about 76 years. Although he did not live to see the success of his prediction of the comet's return in 1758, when the comet was spotted on schedule, it was given his name. Subsequently, at least 23 previous appearances of Halley's comet have been identified from historical records, the first known being from a Chinese text dating from 240BC.

The nucleus is the sole solid component of a comet, and the only part that is always present. It resembles a dark-coloured iceberg; it is a frozen chunk of ice ranging between 5 to 20 km in size, and with a somewhat irregular shape. The ice is not just water ice, but also contains the ices of frozen ammonia, carbon dioxide, methane and carbon monoxide. The ices are blackened, as they contain small fragments of dust embedded within them, and the whole nucleus is of a low density, suggesting it to be a partially porous body. When travelling along the outer reaches of its orbit, far from the Sun, the nucleus remains frozen and dormant. As soon as its path brings the icy block into the inner Solar system, it begins to warm up and its surface becomes active. The solid ice turns directly into gas, in a process known as 'sublimation,' and is liberated from the surface. The process is particularly apparent on the sunward flank of the nucleus, where the gases escape as jets, particularly through any fissures that open up in the structure. These jets also push out the particles of solid dust that are embedded in the ice.

The closer an orbit brings a nucleus to the Sun, the warmer it becomes, and the more spectacular tails are generated with them, sometimes being visible during the day. There are two types of comet tails: dust and gas ion. A dust tail contains small, solid particles that are about the same size as those found in cigarette smoke. This tail forms because sunlight pushes on these small particles, gently shoving them away from the comet's nucleus. Because the pressure from sunlight is relatively weak, the dust particles end up forming a diffuse curved tail in the direction of the comet's orbit. A gas ion tail forms when ultraviolet sunlight rips one or more electrons from gas atoms in the coma, making them into ions. The solar wind then carries these ions straight outward away from the Sun. As a comet heads away from the Sun, its tails dissipate, and the matter contained in its nucleus freezes into a rock-like material.

Glossary

Constellation – a recognised pattern of bodies in the sky.

Elliptical – oval-shaped.

Sublimation - the change of a substance from solid to gas without an intermediate liquid stage.

## Questions 14 – 18

Complete the summary using the words in the box below.

Write your answers in boxes **14 - 18** on your answer sheet.

---

**COMETS**

Comets are quite common in our solar system, but they are seldom (**14**) _____. Comets behave differently to other sky objects; they are seemingly quite (**15**) _____ in their movements and (**16**) _____. Comets have often been seen as predicting (**17**) _____.

Halley's comet is probably the best known 'great comet.' Using previous (**18**) _____, Edmond Halley was successfully able to predict the comet's next appearance, although it occurred after his death.

---

| observations | dangerous | visible | beautiful | naming |
|---|---|---|---|---|
| disaster | success | unpredictable | properties | stars |

## Questions 19 – 23

Complete the sentences below.

Write **NO MORE THAN TWO WORDS** from the text for each answer.

Write your answers in boxes **19 - 23** on your answer sheet.

**19**　　The nucleus of a comet is the only part that is known to be _____ and to remain present through its orbit.

**20**　　The frozen components of a comet's nucleus are _____ due to the presence of dust particles.

**21**　　The nucleus of a comet has been theorised to be porous because of its _____.

**22**　　When far from the sun, a comet's nucleus is icy and _____.

**23**　　Gas jets eject more frequently from the _____ side of a comet.

**Questions 24 – 26**

*Label the diagram below.*

*Write **NO MORE THAN TWO WORDS** from the text for each answer.*

*Write your answers in boxes **24 - 26** on your answer sheet.*

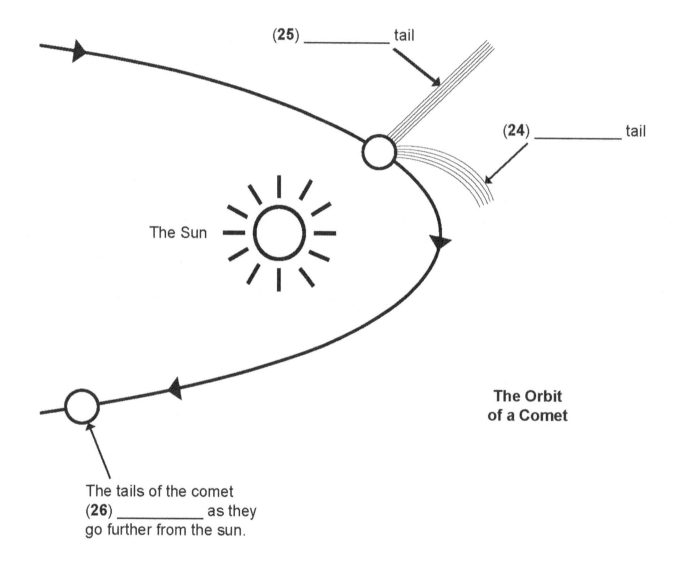

(25) _____ tail

(24) _____ tail

The Sun

**The Orbit
of a Comet**

The tails of the comet
(26) _____ as they
go further from the sun.

## READING PASSAGE 3

*You should spend about 20 minutes on **Questions 27 - 40**, which are based on Reading Passage 3 below*

### US Shale Gas Fracking

**Paragraph A**

We have had widespread drilling for oil and gas deposits for more than 100 years in the United States. Until the 1990's, most of this recovery has occurred from conventional wells that were drilled down to rock formations, from which hydrocarbons could be pumped to the surface. The discovery of hydraulic fracking in the late 1940's has long allowed companies to extract gas and oil from shale, but the perfection of these two techniques over the past few decades has allowed the process to become cost effective. There are numerous shale plays in the United States from which shale gas can be extracted, and firms are busy drilling wells in many areas of the country.

**Paragraph B**

Shale gas is natural methane in rock formations deep underground that, before fracking, was not feasible to extract. Its removal today depends on hydraulic fracturing and horizontal drilling. Hydraulic fracturing is the use of pressure to force liquids containing proppants (often sand) into rock strata, so that hydrocarbons are available for extraction. Current technology uses water, sand, and miscellaneous fluids, all of which must be imported to the well site. A wellbore is drilled, and then the fracturing fluid is forced through holes in the casing into the plays. High pressures are used to create fissures where the proppants are deposited to hold fissures open, so that hydrocarbons can be released. Hydraulic fracturing occurs in a number of stages and the fracturing fluid is forced into a small portion of the wellbore at each stage. After the hydraulic fracturing is completed, some of the fracturing fluid comes back up the well. Because the flowback and wastewater from a well can be toxic, it must be disposed of in a manner that does not create any health, safety, or environmental problems. The underground areas from which the gas is extracted may be left with cavities, which in turn can sometimes cause ground subsidence.

**Paragraph C**

The development of American shale gas deposits has been accompanied by notable benefits and a significant impact on the American economy. Next year, it is estimated that the development of America's shale gas resources will employ 869,000 people. The shale gas industry will have capital expenditures of $48 billion and pay more than $28 billion in federal and state taxes this year. Due to shale gas, the US is using less coal and the country's electricity costs have been lowered by about ten per cent. Shale gas has also contributed to a decrease in imports of foreign natural gas.

**Paragraph D**

Yet not everything is positive. The development of shale gas resources is associated with its toxic pollutants and environmental problems. It needs to be mentioned that the American federal and state governments were not prepared for the problems that accompany shale gas development. A lack of sufficient regulatory oversight in the US when the industry began allowed some unfortunate situations and instances of damage that could have been prevented.

**Paragraph E**

Sites where wells are drilled for extracting shale gas often cover about two hectares and involve increased traffic, noise, light, dangerous equipment, and toxic chemicals. The activities and conditions at a site therefore create a potential for contamination and environmental degradation. The major risk involves damage from the toxic chemicals used in hydraulic fracturing. The fracking fluid is approximately 99.5 per cent water and sand and 0.5 per cent additives used to enhance hydrocarbon recovery. An average of 5000 gallons of chemical additives may be used to frack a well and some of them are toxic. Since different chemicals and different amounts are used at each well, the toxicities may vary.

**Paragraph F**

Under US federal law, the chemicals used at a well are exempted from full reporting requirements. Under most state laws, the supplier or the service company of a fracturing operation must disclose information, unless the chemicals are claimed as a trade secret. Recently, it was estimated that in approximately two-thirds of the cases the complete chemical compositions were not reported. Chemical secrecy is a problem, because persons working at wells and persons who come into contact with chemicals used at a well do not have sufficient information to know whether they need medical attention. Without timely information of the chemicals involved in a spill or release, first responders to emergencies, health professionals, and property owners may lack key information for deciding what actions they should take.

**Paragraph G**

Issues are also being raised about the need for better management practices to reduce the risks that accompany shale gas development. Hundreds of best management practices have been identified to employ during energy development and extraction, but most of these are currently voluntary. In the absence of mandatory management practices covering all of the stages of shale gas development, there are not sufficient assurances that people and the environment are adequately protected against health and safety problems. By adopting more mandatory management practices, the industry may be able to reduce the risks and shale gas development would be beneficial overall.

**Paragraph H**

The American experiences can be helpful in discerning whether other countries might proceed with shale gas development. The activities connected with developing shale gas can be assessed to learn about the risks, dangers, and problems that need to be addressed. Then, existing laws and regulations can be evaluated to determine their probable success in addressing the risks. Additional regulations can be developed if they are needed and firms can be required to adopt best management practices. Governments can require disclosure of dangerous materials and establish funding mechanisms to pay for regulatory oversight and for collecting monies to be used to remedy future damages caused by fracking.

Glossary

Shale play – An underground formation of a type of rock containing natural gas.
Proppant – A solid material used in fracking to keep holes open during the fracking process.

## Questions 27 – 34

*The text above has 8 paragraphs A - H.*

*Which paragraph contains the following information?*

*Write your answers in boxes 27 – 34 on your answer sheet.*

27　　Not all chemicals used for fracking are poisonous.

28　　Shale gas is found deep under the ground.

29　　At present, recommended management practices for fracking companies are not compulsory.

30　　The US government did not initially enforce enough control on the fracking industry.

31　　Fracking techniques have been available since the 1940's.

32　　Finance should be set aside to pay for future problems that fracking might create.

33　　Some companies do not publicise the chemicals that they use for fracking.

34　　Using shale gas has reduced US expenditure on electricity generation.

**Questions 35 – 39**

Choose **FIVE** letters, **A - I**.

Which of the following sentences below accurately describe disadvantages to the US shale gas fracking industry?

Write the correct letter, **A - I**, in any order in boxes **35 - 39** on your answer sheet.

**A**      Toxic liquid can flow up a drilling installation and potentially create pollution.

**B**      Underground gas explosions can be a risk to local communities.

**C**      The ground over the fracking areas can sometimes become unsafe.

**D**      Oil deposits can sometimes be lost during gas fracking.

**E**      Fracking installations generate additional traffic pollution.

**F**      Excess light can be present at fracking installations.

**G**      Sand used in fracking can pollute the water table.

**H**      Workers contaminated during fracking operations can have correct treatment delayed.

**I**      Tax dollars are taken out of the country by overseas extraction companies.

**Question 40**

Choose the correct letter, **A, B, C or D**.

Write the correct letter in box **40** on your answer sheet.

**40**      What is the writer's purpose in Reading Passage 3?

     **A**      To analyse the government's role in US fracking.
     **B**      To criticise US fracking techniques.
     **C**      To compare US and European fracking methods.
     **D**      To provide an overview of the benefits and risks of US fracking.

# WRITING

## WRITING TASK 1

*You should spend about 20 minutes on this task.*

**The images below explain the process of how pollutants from modern life become acid rain that in turn pollutes the environment and the food chain.**

**Summarise the information by selecting and reporting the main features, and make comparisons where relevant.**

*You should write at least 150 words.*

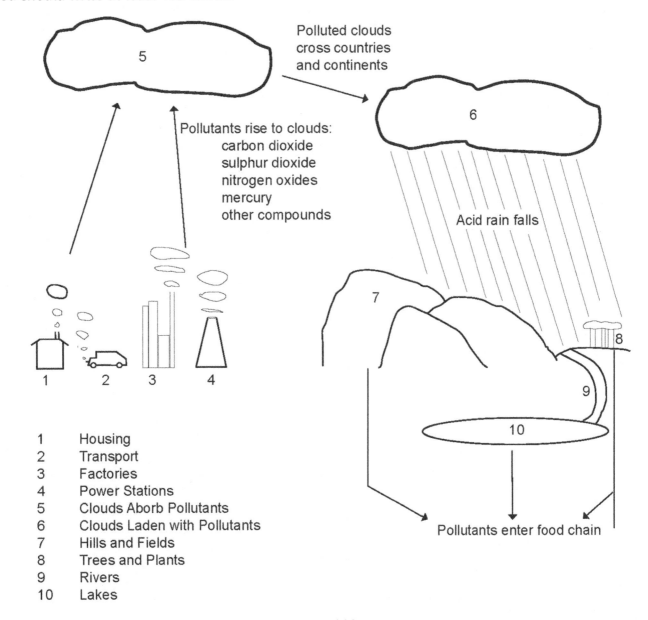

Polluted clouds cross countries and continents

Pollutants rise to clouds:
carbon dioxide
sulphur dioxide
nitrogen oxides
mercury
other compounds

Acid rain falls

Pollutants enter food chain

| | |
|---|---|
| 1 | Housing |
| 2 | Transport |
| 3 | Factories |
| 4 | Power Stations |
| 5 | Clouds Aborb Pollutants |
| 6 | Clouds Laden with Pollutants |
| 7 | Hills and Fields |
| 8 | Trees and Plants |
| 9 | Rivers |
| 10 | Lakes |

## WRITING TASK 2

*You should spend about 40 minutes on this task.*

*Write about the following topic:*

> **Some people believe today that everyone has a right to access to the internet and that governments should provide this access for free. Other people believe that access to the internet is not a right and should be paid for like other services.**
>
> **Discuss both these views and give your opinion.**

*Give reasons for your answer and include any relevant examples from your knowledge or experience.*

*You should write at least 250 words.*

# SPEAKING

## PART 1

- Can you tell me about a shop that is near where you live?
- Who does the shopping in your household?
- Do you prefer shopping in smaller family-owned shops or larger supermarkets? (Why?)

Topic 1        Newspapers and the News
- Do you like to read newspapers? (Why/Why not?)
- Why do people like to be kept up-to-date with the news?
- With the rise of the Internet, do you think paper newspapers will soon be a thing of the past? (Why/Why not?)
- Why is there always a focus on bad news?

Topic 2        Languages
- What languages can you speak?
- Do you think people at school should study a foreign language? (Why/Why not?)
- What are some of the advantages of speaking various languages well?
- Do you think English will keep its importance in the years to come?

## PART 2

```
Describe a memorable party that you went to.
You should say:
        whose party it was
        when the party was
        who was at the party
and explain why this party was so memorable.
```

## PART 3

Topic 1        Celebrations
- What events in your country are celebrated by holding a party?
- What is a polite way of refusing a party invitation?
- What kinds of decisions and considerations are needed when planning a party?
- What are the characteristics of a good host and hostess at a party?

Topic 2        Parties and Alcohol
- What is your viewpoint about people drinking alcohol at a party?
- How should the police deal with people who get out of control at parties because of alcohol?
- How do you think attitudes to alcohol have changed in your country over the last 30 years?
- What can be done to stop young people abusing alcohol?

## Listening Test Answer Sheet

| | | | |
|---|---|---|---|
| 1 | | 21 | |
| 2 | | 22 | |
| 3 | | 23 | |
| 4 | | 24 | |
| 5 | | 25 | |
| 6 | | 26 | |
| 7 | | 27 | |
| 8 | | 28 | |
| 9 | | 29 | |
| 10 | | 30 | |
| 11 | | 31 | |
| 12 | | 32 | |
| 13 | | 33 | |
| 14 | | 34 | |
| 15 | | 35 | |
| 16 | | 36 | |
| 17 | | 37 | |
| 18 | | 38 | |
| 19 | | 39 | |
| 20 | | 40 | |

## Reading Test Answer Sheet

| | | | |
|---|---|---|---|
| 1 | | 21 | |
| 2 | | 22 | |
| 3 | | 23 | |
| 4 | | 24 | |
| 5 | | 25 | |
| 6 | | 26 | |
| 7 | | 27 | |
| 8 | | 28 | |
| 9 | | 29 | |
| 10 | | 30 | |
| 11 | | 31 | |
| 12 | | 32 | |
| 13 | | 33 | |
| 14 | | 34 | |
| 15 | | 35 | |
| 16 | | 36 | |
| 17 | | 37 | |
| 18 | | 38 | |
| 19 | | 39 | |
| 20 | | 40 | |

# Answers

# LISTENING ANSWERS

/ indicates an alternative answer          ( ) indicates an optional answer

| TEST 1 | TEST 2 | TEST 3 | TEST 4 | TEST 5 |
|---|---|---|---|---|
| 1. Simpson | 1. May | 1. 1982 | 1. Easton | 1. Williams |
| 2. 13 | 2. Truman | 2. 30 | 2. 30 | 2. 43 |
| 3. 7RT | 3. 6 p.m. | 3. Wright | 3. October | 3. 1994 |
| 4. 7.30 | 4. Horse riding | 4. 981 | 4. hotels.com | 4. primrose |
| 5. F23 | 5. 30 | 5. Direct debit | 5. Commission | 5. 482 |
| 6. B* | 6. 7 | 6. 2 gigabytes/GB | 6. 13 | 6. A |
| 7. C* | 7. 6 | 7. SIM (card) | 7. sea view | 7. C |
| 8. E* | 8. 5 | 8. 30 | 8. 2,000 | 8. C |
| 9. G* | 9. 400 | 9. 45 | 9. deposit | 9. B |
| 10. K* | 10. 100 | 10. link | 10. Breakfast | 10. B |
| 11. J | 11. L | 11. A* | 11. 1924 | 11. Level 3 |
| 12. F | 12. S | 12. E* | 12. 25 | 12. Level 4 |
| 13. B | 13. F | 13. H* | 13. (health and) safety | 13. Level 7 |
| 14. E | 14. R | 14. K* | 14. ingredients | 14. Level 2 |
| 15. C | 15. A | 15. O* | 15. Wrapping | 15. Level 1 |
| 16. Some fruit | 16. C | 16. residents | 16. lecture | 16. 10 (p.m.) |
| 17. The 2nd floor | 17. C* | 17. 5-minute | 17. guide | 17. The rooftop bar |
| 18. 1 | 18. D* | 18. 4 | 18. 10 | 18. The hotel manager |
| 19. On the terrace | 19. F* | 19. (warming-up) exercises | 19. 13 | 19. At the reception |
| 20. In the restaurant | 20. G* | 20. (bus) driver | 20. wheelchair | 20. By the pool |
| 21. 50% | 21. farmers | 21. C | 21. periods | 21. (town) council |
| 22. cliff formations | 22. field | 22. C | 22. specialisation | 22. car park |
| 23. global warming | 23. growth | 23. B | 23. essays | 23. forecasts |
| 24. hotspots / hot spots | 24. acidity | 24. A | 24. reading | 24. protection |
| 25. overnight | 25. season | 25. B | 25. projects | 25. road access |
| 26. consequences | 26. hard copy | 26. land owner | 26. B* | 26. A |
| 27. foreign students | 27. 30th April | 27. (family) group/family | 27. D* | 27. D |
| 28. 2 hours | 28. 2000 | 28. rangers | 28. F* | 28. B |
| 29. exam | 29. appendices | 29. (big) paths | 29. C | 29. A |
| 30. course tutors | 30. graduate | 30. secret | 30. B | 30. B |
| 31. fat | 31. A | 31. 10,000 | 31. natural dip | 31. China |
| 32. killer whales | 32. C | 32. equipment | 32. clay | 32. trading routes |
| 33. C | 33. C | 33. by-catch | 33. The saturation level | 33. tax |
| 34. A | 34. B | 34. (commercial) (fishing) companies | 34. A (natural) spring | 34. alcohol |
| 35. B | 35. A | 35. B | 35. ecosystems | 35. 6% |
| 36. overfishing | 36. (personality) characteristics | 36. A | 36. urbanisation | 36. Russia |
| 37. 2 degrees | 37. variance | 37. C | 37. evaporates | 37. India |
| 38. nesting areas | 38. guidance | 38. 91 | 38. tap (system) | 38. moisture |
| 39. breeding platforms | 39. shorthand | 39. ecosystems | 39. tanks | 39. cells |
| 40. food | 40. nervous | 40. economies | 40. balance of payments | 40. auctions |
| **Note:** Answers for qu. 6, 7, 8, 9 and 10 can be written in any order | **Note:** Answers for qu. 17, 18, 19 and 20 can be written in any order | **Note:** Answers for qu. 11, 12, 13, 14 and 15 can be written in any order | **Note:** Answers for qu. 26, 27, and 28 can be written in any order | |

# READING ANSWERS

/ indicates an alternative answer        ( ) indicates an optional answer

| TEST 1 | TEST 2 | TEST 3 | TEST 4 | TEST 5 |
|---|---|---|---|---|
| 1. C | 1. research (results) | 1. role of women | 1. FALSE | 1. memory |
| 2. B | 2. layers | 2. patriotism | 2. TRUE | 2. concentration |
| 3. A | 3. duration | 3. resources | 3. NOT GIVEN | 3. infants |
| 4. D | 4. mercury | 4. radioactivity | 4. TRUE | 4. proportion |
| 5. A | 5. cars | 5. minerals | 5. TRUE | 5. epilepsy |
| 6. NO | 6. Cold War | 6. origin | 6. clay | 6. immune system |
| 7. NOT GIVEN | 7. breakthrough | 7. exposure | 7. tempering wheel | 7. energy |
| 8. YES | 8. patent | 8. E | 8. moulds | 8. TRUE |
| 9. NOT GIVEN | 9. reliability | 9. C | 9. sand | 9. NOT GIVEN |
| 10. D | 10. indicator | 10. D | 10. strength | 10. FALSE |
| 11. C | 11. A vinegar solution | 11. F | 11. kiln | 11. FALSE |
| 12. F | 12. An iron rod | 12. A | 12. leaves | 12. TRUE |
| 13. A | 13. Copper wire | 13. B | 13. 20 millimetres | 13. NOT GIVEN |
| 14. E | 14. DC | 14. A sluice gate | 14. C | 14. visible |
| 15. C | 15. JB | 15. A turbine | 15. A | 15. unpredictable |
| 16. G | 16. CA | 16. B | 16. C | 16. properties |
| 17. A | 17. DW | 17. A | 17. B | 17. disaster |
| 18. F | 18. PE | 18. F | 18. D | 18. observations |
| 19. D | 19. CA | 19. D | 19. C | 19. solid |
| 20. B | 20. MH | 20. expenditure | 20. spending | 20. blackened |
| 21. Tourism | 21. DW | 21. nuclear power | 21. disposable incomes | 21. low density |
| 22. Pesticides | 22. critical thinker | 22. (tidal) flows | 22. Governments | 22. dormant |
| 23. Around a decade | 23. self-censor | 23. climate | 23. landscapes | 23. sunward |
| 24. Temperature | 24. personal | 24. weather | 24. region | 24. dust |
| 25. Glaciers melting | 25. opportunities | 25. water levels | 25. rural economies | 25. gas ion |
| 26. Local people | 26. C | 26. lock | 26. fresh farm goods | 26. dissipate |
| 27. TRUE | 27. iv | 27. SM | 27. E | 27. E |
| 28. FALSE | 28. vi | 28. AM | 28. C | 28. B |
| 29. NOT GIVEN | 29. ii | 29. AH | 29. F | 29. G |
| 30. effectiveness | 30. i | 30. KS | 30. B | 30. D |
| 31. intrusion | 31. viii | 31. JH | 31. G | 31. A |
| 32. dramatic moments | 32. ix | 32. TW | 32. A | 32. H |
| 33. familiarity | 33. v | 33. CC | 33. D | 33. F |
| 34. unwilling | 34. C | 34. YES | 34. formalin | 34. C |
| 35. celebrities | 35. A | 35. NO | 35. mutation | 35. A* |
| 36. Consumers | 36. C | 36. NOT GIVEN | 36. trials | 36. C* |
| 37. pressure | 37. B | 37. NO | 37. variant | 37. E* |
| 38. adjustment | 38. TRUE | 38. YES | 38. Children | 38. F* |
| 39. mood | 39. NOT GIVEN | 39. NO | 39. 70% | 39. H* |
| 40. term | 40. FALSE | 40. B | 40. Refugees | 40. D |
|  |  |  |  | **Note**: Answers for qu. 35, 36, 37, 38 + 39 can be written in any order |

# READING ANSWERS HELP

This section shows fragments of passages that contain the correct answers. If you have trouble locating the correct answer in the text, or can't understand why a particular answer is correct, refer to this section to understand the reasoning behind the answers. A group of answers with answers being preceded by * means that this group of answers may be given in any order. Answers in brackets () are optional answers.

## ACADEMIC READING TEST 1

1. **C**     Research affirms the importance of second language education regarding intellectual potential, scholastic achievement, first language skills, citizenship and the economy.

2. **B**     Educational research shows that results in English and Science are better for students who study one. The reasons for this are not altogether clear:

3. **A**     People who are multilingual are proficient at slipping from one language system to another and using totally different language mechanics. This is very distracting and demanding work, not only for the tongue and language faculties, but also especially for the brain.

4. **D**     People who have developed this are highly proficient multi-taskers and commit very few errors when juggling various activities.

5. **A**     several pieces of research have also shown that multilingual adults experienced the onset of Alzheimer's and dementia at a later age of 75 compared to monolingual adults, who had the first signs at age 71.

6. **NO**          The studies were conducted with other variables such as gender, overall health, educational level, and economic status, but there were no significant results that contributed to the mentioned diseases as significantly as the number of languages spoken.

7. **NOT GIVEN**    There is nothing in the text relating to this and so the answer is 'not given' in the text.

8. **YES**          Businesses are of course interested in people who have an ability that improves their intelligence, flexibility, openness to diverse people, and decision-making skills.

9. **NOT GIVEN**         There is nothing in the text relating to this and so the answer is 'not given' in the text.

10. **D**   Finally, self-confidence is a normal consequence of learning a new language.

11. **C**   people tend to gravitate around multilingual people because of their skills; others simply find the openness and quick-mindedness of multi-lingual people naturally attractive.

12. **F**   the ability to explore a culture through its native tongue or talk to someone with whom it might otherwise not be able to communicate.

Page 126

13. **A**    Learning a second language is best introduced at the earliest age possible, but learning it at a much later age is still very much worthwhile.

14. **E**    Cyclones can have devastating effects on the Great Barrier Reef, the immediate effect being the physical damage. Fast maturing coral is easily destroyed by storms

15. **C**    Freshwater flood plumes can have a number of effects, including killing coral at shallow depths.

16. **G**    A lesser-known problem is that earth or residue that is carried out to sea can affect coral growing in the deep water, as it can block out the light that coral needs to survive.

17. **A**    Even relatively small increases in ocean acidity decrease the capacity of corals to build skeletons, which in turn decreases their capacity to create living environments for the Reef's marine life.

18. **F**    On coral reefs, temperature changes affect the relationship of mutual dependence between some animals and the algae that live within their tissues.

19. **D**    large changes in sea levels can mean land inundation, which will cause significant changes in tidal habitats, such as saltwater intrusion into low-lying freshwater habitats like mangroves.

20. **B**    Reefs will probably be able to accommodate a sea level rise of three millimetres

21. **Tourism**    It also is a major source of income to people near the Reef, with tourism now being the key industry in the local towns.

22. **Pesticides**        Large scale flooding can carry various land-based pollutants, such as fertilisers, herbicides and the worst, pesticides, out to the Reef, which can have a devastating effect.

23. **Around a decade**        Although the chemistry is simple and well understood, its effect on marine life is much less well known, as the process has only been recognised for around a decade.

24. **Temperature**        Temperature is a key environmental factor controlling the distribution and diversity of marine life; it is critical to reef building and controls the rate of coral reef growth more than anything.

25. **Glaciers melting**        Sea levels on the Great Barrier Reef have already risen by approximately three millimetres per year since 1991, due to a combination of thermal expansion in the oceans and, most significantly, glaciers melting.

26. **Local people**        It seems that local people are motivated to change in order to protect the Great Barrier Reef

27. **TRUE**        Since the Ancient Greeks, music has been recognised as a powerful emotional force. They believed that music was such a powerful force that it could stir men into bravery on the battlefields or it could impose moral order and civilising harmony on unruly pupils.

28. **FALSE**      Mass advertising using soundtracks began in the 1920's and 1930's with commercial radio in the United States

29. **NOT GIVEN**      There is nothing in the text relating to this and so the answer is 'not given' in the text.

30. **effectiveness**      Good music can contribute to the effectiveness of an advertisement merely by making it more attractive.

31. **intrusion**      Music serves to engage listeners' attention and render the advertisement less of an unwanted intrusion.

32. **dramatic moments**      Historically originating in film music, advertising music can also be structurally employed as simply an uninterrupted background, or to heighten or highlight dramatic moments.

33. **familiarity**      A third important function for music is to intensify the familiarity of a product.

34. **unwilling**      Surprisingly, such musical lingering may occur even when the mind is an unwilling host.

35. **celebrities**      Indeed, it may be the case that effective targeting is merely the result of the formation of proper authority. A simple way of creating this is through specialist testimony or employing celebrities.

36. **Consumers**      However, over periods of time, consumers become resistant to the means by which advertisers establish authority.

37. **pressure**      The role of music in advertising recognises that music is a really powerful tool for selling things and this success has created added responsibilities to those people who wish to become music composers.

38. **adjustment**      In the 1930's, the rise of films with soundtracks led to a new type of commission for composers, where they had to tailor their music to a film scenario, to its narrative pace, and to the emotions of a character.

39. **mood**      film and TV composers have written so-called library music, where their soundtrack is categorised by describing its emotional evocation, and can be used in a variety of programmes. Viewers may have had the experience of watching a television programme and thinking, "I actually recognise that music from a previous series or a completely different programme."

40. **term**      music will then be reused whenever the producer of a film or a TV programme enters those particular emotional keywords into the database of library music.

## ACADEMIC READING TEST 2

1. **research (results)**      Luigi Galvani, another Italian scientist and contemporary of Volta, almost made the discovery, but misinterpreted his research results.

2. **layers**      Volta's battery was made by piling up layers of silver and paper or cloth, soaked in salt, and zinc.

3. **duration**      Volta's battery was not good for delivering currents for any significant duration.

4. **mercury**      John Daniell used a copper pot, copper sulphate, sulphuric acid and mercury to produce his electric current. Although we now know better than to put mercury into batteries

5. **cars**      the lead acid battery is one that stands out. First made in 1859, it was further improved in 1881 and this design even now forms the basis of the modern lead acid battery found in cars.

6. **Cold War**      One very common battery used today is the lithium-ion battery, which was developed by the United States' Central Intelligence Agency (CIA) as a part of their efforts during the Cold War.

7. **breakthrough**      In the early 1960's, both the private and public sectors were experimenting with creating batteries using lithium, but the breakthrough in the chemistry was achieved by adding the ion into the equation.

8. **patent**      Not long after its invention, the CIA shared the lithium-ion battery concept with the public and a company working on an exploratory project developed and created the first patent for the lithium-ion battery for commercial use in 1968.

9. **reliability**      Today, the lithium-ion battery is the most common type of battery used in pacemakers, because of its reliability and life span.

10. **indicator**      Because of the battery's decreasing voltage, electrical designers can design an indicator for the pacemaker that allows the device to inform the doctor a new battery is needed.

11. **A vinegar solution**      Dating back 2,000 years, the 'battery' would have comprised a clay jar filled with a vinegar solution.

12. **An iron rod**      An iron rod was put into the middle of the jar and encircled with copper wire.

13. **Copper wire**      An iron rod was put into the middle of the jar and encircled with copper wire.

14. **DC**      Don Croft, a parent of a six-year-old boy, recently wrote ... about how his child should not follow the examples he read about in this particular book.

15. **JB**      A lot of people want to control everything in their children's lives, or everything in other people's children's lives.

16. **CA**      Carol Anderson explains that there are several good reasons. "The exposure to different authors and genres of books can give your child insight into other societies, worldwide locations, and new vocabulary.

17. **DW**      Wooten is also concerned with other issues. "There is decreased readership among children and young adults because of digital distractions."

18. **PE**      A lot of parents don't have reading as a tradition and there aren't any books they would suggest their children read.

19. **CA**      They are a great starting point to introduce children to the concept of a story and to introduce them to different types of stories or genres.

20. **MH**      As long as the students are able to develop the skill of visualising what they are reading, they are learning.

21. **DW**      Children learn how language and writing work, even when reading books dismissed by some as piffle, says Wooten.

22. **critical thinker**      Another point of view is that 'low quality literature' can give the opportunity to teach a child to be a critical thinker

23. **self-censor**      If a book is really unsuitable, the children themselves will simply self-censor themselves.

24. **personal**      There is a growing body of evidence that emphasises the importance of reading for pleasure, for both educational purposes as well as personal development.

25. **opportunities**      Children who read very little do not have the benefits that come with reading, and studies show that when struggling readers are not motivated to read, their opportunities to gain knowledge decrease significantly.

26 **C**      This is a holistic answer and involves synthesis of the whole text. This text in its entirety fits "To discuss whether all reading can be beneficial for children" better than the other three answers.

27. **iv**      Various information within Paragraph A.

28. **vi**      Various information within Paragraph B.

29. **ii**      Various information within Paragraph C.

30. **i**          Various information within Paragraph D.

31. **viii**       Various information within Paragraph E.

32. **ix**         Various information within Paragraph F.

33. **v**          Various information within Paragraph G.

34. **C**          The name 'Spanish' influenza merely reflects that Spain, which was neutral in World War 1, did not censor their news agencies from publicising the severity of the pandemic in the country, and this made it seem to other countries that the disease was worse there.

35. **A**          These three extensive pandemic waves of influenza within one year, occurring in rapid succession, with only the briefest of quieter intervals between them, were unprecedented.

36. **C**          The world economy as a whole was not significantly affected

37. **B**          Those who survived that pandemic and lived to experience the 1918 pandemic tended to be less susceptible to the disease and so a lot more Americans lived than would have otherwise been the case.

38. **TRUE**       Influenza hit areas quickly and often, but it disappeared within a few weeks of its arrival. Many people did not have time to fully realise just how great was the danger.

39. **NOT GIVEN**       There is nothing in the text relating to this and so the answer is 'not given' in the text.

40. **FALSE**      Ironically, the health of the young adults made them the most affected.

## ACADEMIC READING TEST 3

1. **role of women**     Her life offers insights into the changing role of women in science and academia over the past century.

2. **patriotism**     Although Marie's family was not wealthy, both parents were teachers and instilled in their children a love of learning and a deep patriotism, which led to her opposing the Russian occupation of her country.

3. **resources**     Both the sisters realised that individually, they did not have enough resources to enable them to go to Paris, so they decided that one of them would go first by pulling their resources together.

4. **radioactivity**     Pierre and Marie married and began their historic collaboration on the nature of radioactivity at a small institute out of the mainstream of the scientific establishment.

5. **minerals**     Marie found that two uranium minerals, pitchblende and chalcocite, were more active than uranium itself, so she hypothesised that a new element that was considerably more active than uranium was present in small amounts.

6. **origin**     By July 1903, they had isolated a new element, and they wrote, "We propose to call it polonium after the name of the country of origin of one of us."

7. **exposure**     Over the next 20 or so years, Marie worked with radioactive elements and, because the dangers of working with them were not fully understood at that time, the long exposure led to her sickness and death from a type of leukaemia at the age of 66.

8. **E**     In 1890, Bronya graduated and a year later, Marie began her university degree in Paris.

9. **C**     In 1896, Becquerel had shown that uranium compounds, even if they were kept in the dark, emitted rays that would fog a photographic plate. This was an accidental discovery

10. **D**     Both the new elements were much more radioactive than uranium and their discoveries brought the Curies international fame with the awarding of the Nobel Prize in 1903.

11. **F**     Following Pierre's death in a road accident in 1906

12. **A**     her application for membership in the Academy of Sciences in 1910 was rejected

13. **B**     Marie received her second Nobel Prize in 1911.

14. **A sluice gate**     This dam has a number of underwater tunnels cut into its width allowing seawater to flow through them in a controllable way, using a sluice gate on the sea and reservoir side, which can slide down or up to release or retain water as desired.

15. **A turbine**  Fixed within the tunnels are propellers that are turned by the tidal flow and they in turn spin a turbine.

16. **B**              Other disadvantages of a tidal barrage system are the high construction costs and the environmental effects that a long concrete dam may have on the estuary it spans.

17. **A**              A tidal stream generation system reduces some of the environmental effects of tidal barrages by using turbine generators beneath the surface of the water.

18. **F**              Tidal stream generation is very similar in principal to wind power generation, except this time, water currents flow across a turbine's rotor blades that rotate the turbine, much like how wind currents turn the blades for wind power turbines. In fact, tidal stream generation areas on the seabed can look just like underwater wind farms.

19. **D**              As water is much denser than air and has a much slower flow rate, tidal stream turbines have much smaller diameters and higher tip speed rates compared to an equivalent wind turbine.

20. **expenditure**         The building expenditure was significant, even back in 1966 when it was opened, but these have now been recovered

21. **nuclear power**           electricity production costs are lower than that of nuclear power.

22. **(tidal) flows**      The tidal flows are regulated in the estuary by the operators, who adjust them to minimise the biological impact.

23. **climate**              It has no impact on climate, because it does not emit any greenhouse gases.

24. **weather**   The pattern of the tides is preserved, so that the impact on species living in the estuary is minimal. The operator monitors the tides and weather forecasts to program the barrage operations on a weekly basis.

25. **water levels**      The water levels in the lagoon are higher than it was before the construction, which has promoted an increase in boating and sailing activities.

26. **lock**      The facility attracts approximately 70,000 visitors per year and a canal lock in the west end of the dam permits the passage of 20,000 vessels each year between the English Channel and the Rance.

27. **SM**      The researcher in charge of the study, Sophie Meaker, comments on the results. "While our study gives us some data to help guide our actions with regard to reoffending, they are still not accurate enough for determining life-altering decisions with respect to individuals."

28. **AM**      Prosecutor Angela Martin comments on this case. "While prison might please the relatives of those killed, it is unnecessary for the protection of society and expensive to the taxpayer. I believe the only proper use of prison is for the containment of dangerous criminals, including violent men and serial burglars who cannot be reformed."

29. **AH**    Parole officer, Alison Headley, opposes tagging for almost an opposite reason. "Tagging is a soft option and one that most prisoners, especially re-offenders, would prefer. It does not punish sufficiently or effectively and does not discourage re-offending."

30. **KS**    Prison director, Katherine Soames, … has mixed feelings
As for rehabilitation, prisons stigmatise people, sever family ties and make it more difficult to get employment on release."

31. **JH**    Jason Howell, a judge in Australia, is a fan. "It is better than short-term prison sentences at reducing reoffending and allows monitoring without a prison sentence.

32. **TW**    Activist Tom Wilkinson argues that tagging should be illegal. "Tagging clearly contravenes a couple of basic human rights, such as the right not to undergo degrading treatment or the right to a private family life.

33. **CC**    Ministry of Justice executive, Colin Case, explains some facts. "Recidivism figures give little cause for optimism regarding the effectiveness of short- or medium-term prison sentences.

34. **YES**    There seems to be confusion as to what exactly prison is for.

35. **NO**    One possible more humane alternative to prison and one of the best is community service. This has elements of punishment (deprivation of freedom and some degree of humiliation)

36. **NOT GIVEN**    There is nothing in the text relating to this and so the answer is 'not given' in the text.

37. **NO**    A control centre can monitor the whereabouts and movements of anyone wearing a tag. This can and ought to be used as a sentence in itself or part of an early release system.

38. **YES**    When taking this into account, it seems that tagging is not a suitable measure for re-offenders.

39. **NO**    Prison will continue to be widely used

40. **B**    This is a holistic answer and involves synthesis of the whole text. This text in its entirety fits "Prison and its Alternatives" better than the other three answers.

## ACADEMIC READING TEST 4

1. **FALSE**        Fired brick are also useful in hotter climates, as they can absorb any heat generated throughout the day and then release it at night.

2. **TRUE**        The Romans were real brick connoisseurs. They preferred to make their bricks in the spring

3. **NOT GIVEN**        There is nothing in the text relating to this and so the answer is 'not given' in the text.

4. **TRUE**        Bricks suffered a setback during the Renaissance and Baroque periods, with exposed brick walls becoming unpopular and brickwork being generally covered by plaster.

5. **TRUE**        On the other hand, there are some bricks that are more porous and therefore more susceptible to damage from dampness when exposed to water.

6. **clay**        The process involves putting the clay, water and additives into a large pit, where it is all mixed together by a tempering wheel

7. **tempering wheel**        The process involves putting the clay, water and additives into a large pit, where it is all mixed together by a tempering wheel

8. **moulds**        Once the mixture is of the correct consistency, the clay is removed and pressed into moulds by hand.

9. **sand**        To prevent the brick from sticking to the mould, the brick is coated in either sand or water, though coating a brick with sand gives an overall better finish to it.

10. **strength**        If these bricks left outside for the drying process are exposed to a shower, the water can leave indentations on the brick, which, although not affecting the strength of the brick, is considered very undesirable.

11. **kiln**        After drying, the bricks are then transferred to the kiln for firing and this creates the finished product.

12. **leaves**        This is primarily achieved today through cavity wall insulation. Insulating bricks are built in two separate leaves, as they are called in the trade. The gap between the inner and outer leaves of brickwork depends on the type of insulation used

13. **20 millmetres**        The gap between the inner and outer leaves of brickwork depends on the type of insulation used, but there should be enough space for a gap of twenty millimetres between the insulating material in the cavity and the two leaves on either side.

14. **C**        In addition, there has been added public pressure to make expensive changes in farming methods, due to public environmental concerns about industrialised agricultural production

15. **A**     in combination with political pressures to reduce agricultural subsidies.

16. **C**     Some farmers are offering their barns as venues for weddings, parties, dances and other special events.

17. **B**     For one thing, the image of the family farm remains imbued with deep authenticity, the surviving representation of an old world ideal. To partake in agritourism is therefore likely to convey the sense of having a deeply authentic experience.

18. **D**     It seems therefore that often the most distinctive innovative effort involves the reinvention of tradition and rural tourism products. Examples are the recreation of home-produced products long since replaced by manufactured commodities and the provision of hands-on-experiences in crafts often recreated for tourists.

19. **C**     As a result, some critics argue that the tourists who are running to the countryside are over-crowding and ruining the pristine beauty that they so desperately want to experience.

20. **spending**     This means that tourist spending on agritourism often stays in the region

21. **disposable incomes**     This means that tourist spending on agritourism often stays in the region, helping it by generating taxable income and more disposable incomes.

22. **Governments**     This, in turn, helps governments by keeping farmers on land, protecting picturesque rural landscapes that attract tourists

23. **landscapes**     This, in turn, helps governments by keeping farmers on land, protecting picturesque rural landscapes that attract tourists,

24. **region**     This, in turn, helps governments by keeping farmers on land, protecting picturesque rural landscapes that attract tourists, and supporting the production of agricultural products from the region.

25. **rural economies**     Agritourism contributes to and enhances the quality of life in communities by expanding recreational opportunities, differentiating rural economies

26. **fresh farm goods**     Finally, many agritourism operations provide consumers with direct access to fresh farm goods.

27. **E**     OPV is taken by mouth and, like a wild poliovirus, induces immunity against itself in the gut wall as it travels through the intestine.

28. **C**     This fear of polio was deliberately fuelled and exploited by the March of Dimes, an American fund-raising organisation set up by President Franklin D Roosevelt, himself a polio survivor.

29. **F**    Sabin's OPV, being cheaper, more effective and easier to give, later superseded the Salk vaccine.

30. **B**    Each year, panic resurfaced as the polio season approached, with the wealthy leaving towns and cities in droves.

31. **G**    Tragically, though, endemic polio continues to cling on in three areas, Afghanistan, Pakistan and Northern Nigeria, largely because of anti-western ideology that is backed up by intimidation, death threats and the murder of many vaccinators and their supporters.

32. **A**    The iron lung, which was officially known as a negative pressure ventilator, was invented hundreds of years ago, but was further developed in the 1930's to help with the world polio outbreaks. At one point, the need for iron lungs was so high that they were used with a patient within an hour of their manufacture.

33. **D**    Less dramatic were massive doses of vitamins C and chemically modified cobra venom.

34. **formalin**    Jonas Salk (1914–1998) favoured an 'inactivated polio vaccine' (IPV), in which wild polioviruses are 'killed' with formalin, so that they can no longer replicate and spread into the spinal cord.

35. **mutation**    The 'oral polio vaccine' (OPV) developed by Albert Sabin (1906–1993) relies on the fact that polioviruses forced to grow under unfavourable conditions in the laboratory will undergo mutation into forms that can no longer invade the spinal cord.

36. **trials**    Salk's IPV was the first polio vaccine to be tested on a large scale, in massive clinical trials in 1954 involving 1.8 million American children. Following the sensational declaration that his vaccine 'works and is safe', Salk became a national and international hero, and mass vaccination of children with his IPV began immediately.

37. **variant**    There is an exceedingly low risk (one in 500,000 vaccinations) of Sabin's OPV reverting to a paralysing variant, a drawback that Sabin always refused to acknowledge.

38. **Children**    Polio originally caused sporadic clusters of paralysis, especially in children.

39. **70%**    the iron lung itself carried considerable risks. Until chest infections could be properly treated, seventy per cent of patients put inside the iron lung died there.

40. **Refugees countries**    Usually refugees, but also other travellers, have reintroduced polio to other

## ACADEMIC READING TEST 5

1. **memory**    We need sleep for biological restoration. It promotes cell growth, regeneration and memory consolidation.

2. **concentration**    When people are deprived of sleep for any reason, there is deterioration in performance, particularly on tasks requiring concentration, and eventually, behaviour becomes shambolic.

3. **infants**    Infants spend up to 50 per cent of their sleep time in REM sleep, which is understandable when one realises that REM sleep is the time used for brain development, as well as learning, thinking, and organising information.

4. **proportion**    If people are woken when REM sleep commences, depriving them specifically of dream-sleep, the proportion of REM sleep increases once they fall asleep again to make up what was lost.

5. **epilepsy**    Sleep also affects some kinds of epilepsy in complex ways.

6. **immune system**    The neurons that control sleep interact strongly with the immune system. As anyone who has had the flu knows, infectious diseases tend to make people feel sleepy.

7. **energy**    Sleep helps the body conserve energy that the body's immune system needs to mount an attack.

8. **TRUE**    Sleep deprivation is an effective therapy for people with certain types of depression, while it can actually cause depression in other people.

9. **NOT GIVEN**    There is nothing in the text relating to this and so the answer is 'not given' in the text

10. **FALSE**    Patients who are unable to sleep also notice pain more and may increase their requests for pain medication.

11. **FALSE**    Insomnia is a widespread affliction.

12. **TRUE**    When insomniacs are observed in a sleep lab, their EEG records often suggest that their sleep pattern is fairly normal, even though in the morning they maintain they hardly slept a wink.

13. **NOT GIVEN**    There is nothing in the text relating to this and so the answer is 'not given' in the text.

14. **visible**    only comparatively rarely do they reach sufficient brightness to become apparent to the unaided eye.

15. **unpredictable**    A planet follows a fairly slow but expected path. By comparison, a comet is a totally different kind of event: it will appear unexpectedly and at any place in the sky, it will change position from one night to the next relative to the background of stars, and its path will be along a separate direction and path across the sky from the planets and stars.

Page 138

16. **properties**        During the few weeks or months that it is observable, it will first steadily increase in brightness from one night to the next, may change its shape – growing bigger, longer or extra tails – and then wane to invisibility, never to be seen again.

17. **disaster**        Throughout history, comets have always signified evil, war and death, and they were supposed to leave chaos and calamity in their wake. Indeed, plenty of past comets have been blamed by the astrologers of their day for bringing or marking misfortune.

18. **observations**        During the 17th century, Halley was using Newton's new mathematics of calculus to try to characterise the orbits of twenty-four comets from observations recorded over the previous four centuries.

19. **solid**        The nucleus is the sole solid component of a comet

20. **blackened**        The ices are blackened, as they contain small fragments of dust embedded within them

21. **low density**        the whole nucleus is of a low density, suggesting it to be a partially porous body.

22. **dormant**        When travelling along the outer reaches of its orbit, far from the Sun, the nucleus remains frozen and dormant.

23. **sunward**        The process is particularly apparent on the sunward flank of the nucleus, where the gases escape as jets

24. **dust**        Because the pressure from sunlight is relatively weak, the dust particles end up forming a diffuse curved tail in the direction of the comet's orbit.

25. **gas ion**        A gas ion tail forms when ultraviolet sunlight rips one or more electrons from gas atoms in the coma, making them into ions. The solar wind then carries these ions straight outward away from the Sun.

26. **dissipate**        As a comet heads away from the Sun, its tails dissipate

27. **E**        An average of 5000 gallons of chemical additives may be used to frack a well and some of them are toxic.

28. **B**        Shale gas is natural methane in rock formations deep underground that, before fracking, was not feasible to extract.

29. **G**        Hundreds of best management practices have been identified to employ during energy development and extraction, but most of these are currently voluntary.

30. **D**    A lack of sufficient regulatory oversight when the industry began allowed some unfortunate situations and instances of damage that could have been prevented.

31. **A**    The discovery of hydraulic fracking in the late 1940's has long allowed companies to extract gas and oil from shale

32. **H**    Governments can require disclosure of dangerous materials and establish funding mechanisms to pay for regulatory oversight and for collecting monies to be used to remedy future damages caused by fracking.

33. **F**    Recently, it was estimated that in approximately two-thirds of the cases the complete chemical compositions were not reported.

34. **C**    Due to shale gas, the US is using less coal and the country's electricity costs have been lowered by about ten per cent.

35. **A***    After the hydraulic fracturing is completed, some of the fracturing fluid comes back up the well. Because the flowback and wastewater from a well can be toxic, it must be disposed of in a manner that does not create any health, safety, or environmental problems.

36. **C***    The underground areas from which the gas is extracted may be left with cavities, which in turn can sometimes cause ground subsidence.

37. **E***    Sites where wells are drilled for extracting shale gas often cover about two hectares and involve increased traffic

38. **F***    Sites where wells are drilled for extracting shale gas often cover about two hectares and involve increased traffic, noise, light

39. **H***    Without timely information of the chemicals involved in a spill or release, first responders to emergencies, health professionals, and property owners may lack key information for deciding what actions they should take.

40. **D**    This is a holistic answer and involves synthesis of the whole text. This text in its entirety fits the answer "To provide an overview of the benefits and risks of US fracking" better than the other three answers.

# EXAMPLE WRITING ANSWERS

Below you will find example writing answers for all the writing questions in the Academic Practice Tests 1 to 5. There are many ways of answering the writing questions and these examples are only one possibility of a good answer. Please refer to the question papers while you are reading these reports and essays so that you understand the questions that are being answered. We hope this will give you an insight into how the writing answers should be written for IELTS Academic module.

## ACADEMIC WRITING PRACTICE TEST 1

### Task 1

This report will describe a bar chart showing the average rainfall for Australia last year by month and the average rainfall in Australia for the past forty years.

Overall, it can be seen that the average rainfall for Australia last year was a little lower than the average rainfall in Australia for the past forty years, but it generally followed the same pattern.

The average rainfall of the last forty years in Australia decreased from a peak at the beginning of the year to lows in the months in the middle of the year. Towards the end of the year, rainfall rose again. Rainfall data for last year generally followed the same trend as the last forty years' average.

Although the general pattern of the two sets of data is similar, there are some differences. The line representing the accumulation of the average rainfall from the past forty years begins at around eighty millimetres in January and then drops sharply to around thirty millimetres in April. Rainfall then drops slowly to around thirteen millimetres in September and then again rises steadily to just under sixty millimetres in December. Average rainfall for the last forty years was a little lower than average for most months, excepting March, May, June and November when the rainfall was a little heavier. August and October were particularly dry when compared with the forty-year average, at around five millimetres each, compared with about fifteen and twenty millimetres each respectively for the forty-year average.                    (247 words)

**Task 2**

In schools, students learn to analyse literature, calculate using trigonometry and understand how photosynthesis works, but often students are inexperienced and helpless after graduation when encountering the real world. It is therefore argued that schools should teach their students how to survive financially in the world.

This topic is difficult though. Many educators believe that a school is supposed to teach students in subjects that they will most probably not encounter again post graduation, so that teachers can develop open-minded and well-informed individuals. At the same time though, it can be argued that schools should impart skills that would be applicable in every day life. Mathematics, for example, is supposed to not only communicate actual mathematics skills, but also teach logic to students. However, schools are supposed to prepare the youths for their lives following high school. Currently this goal is not fully met, as often students are unable to handle their finances sensibly and therefore can often face significant problems. Schools that teach students how to survive financially could change this.

This significant shift in the ideology of education is unlikely to take place soon, as the education system has been in place for too long to be easily changed. Also a change of this scale would be costly, as teachers would have to be trained and a syllabus for this potential subject would have to be created. However, in some countries, for example Germany, a community subject is available in which politics and finances are discussed. This leaves students from Germany in a better situation to deal with finances in their lives.

In conclusion, training school students in financial matters would be very useful. Adding new content to the syllabus would require a significant amount of money, but the entire community would benefit from students being better prepared for adult life.          *(303 words)*

## ACADEMIC WRITING PRACTICE TEST 2

### Task 1

The two pie charts show the amount of electricity generated by energy source in Scotland for twenty years ago and last year.

Overall, it can be seen that the various sources of energy used in Scotland and the amount of energy gained from each of them have not significantly changed when comparing the values from last year and twenty years ago.

In a noticeably similar way, Scotland generated the greatest amount of electricity from coal in the past and recently, with 41.4% being generated twenty years ago and 32.7% being generated last year. The other sources of the energy generation, however, have spread out more, when looking at last year's data.

Compared to twenty years ago, Scotland has made slight changes to its reliance on certain sources for the generation of electricity. Although the major generator remains as coal (followed again by gas), there has been an increase in the use of oil (from 2.1% to 4.0%), nuclear energy (from 19.6% to 26.4%) and other renewable sources (from 2.8% to 5.1%). The most significant changes would be to the use of oil and other renewable sources, as the use of these two sources last year was almost double the percentage of electricity that was being generated from them twenty years ago.                    (211 words)

### Task 2

The population of the world is ever growing. Some people believe that this increase has created an unsustainable situation and that it will lead to a global crisis. Other people believe that only through an increasing population can the world's economy and society develop.

This population increase is not constant around the world; population is undergoing significant growth especially in less developed countries, and the continent of Africa is predicted to undergo the highest increase. Many people living in these less developed countries frequently face shortages, such as water, food, heating, cooking fuel and medicines, and people have to live in substandard living conditions by western standards. With more inhabitants, these difficulties will become exacerbated and helping these countries might also create strain on the resources and economies of other countries.

On the other hand, many countries are unable to reach their economic potential due to a lack of skilled work forces. For these countries a growing population can mean a stronger economy and, due to that, a better standard of living. Growing populations can also lead to growing demand for goods, allowing economies to expand. The problem is, however, that countries that are in need of labour forces and increasing demand are already the more developed countries and they meet some of these needs by immigration and exporting goods.

In conclusion, it is my belief that while certain areas of the world are in need of larger work forces to develop their economies, the continuously increasing population could potentially lead to crisis within countries that already struggle to provide for their inhabitants.

*(263 words)*

Page 143

## ACADEMIC WRITING PRACTICE TEST 3

### Task 1

The two tables compare from last year the number of workers in the US that were of US birth to the number of workers who were of foreign birth. The tables include divisions of the workforce by gender and by age, summarising the total number of workers in the workforce, the number of employed and unemployed workers and finally the unemployment rate. All figures are in thousands.

Overall, it can be seen that in spite of the much larger numbers involved with the US birth workforce, the total unemployment rates were quite similar for the two cohorts.

When looking at the breakdown of the figures by gender, the male foreign birth workforce suffered a lower unemployment rate (8.9%) than the male US birth workforce (10.6%), whereas the female foreign birth workforce suffered a higher unemployment rate (11.1%) than the female US birth workforce (8.5%). Overall, the male foreign birth workforce suffered a marginally higher rate of unemployment (9.8%) than the US birth workforce (9.6%). The total US birth workforce in size was significantly larger (129,533 people) than the total foreign birth workforce (24,357 people).

When looking at the breakdown of the figures by age, the younger of the foreign birth workforce (16 – 24 and 25 – 34) suffered from lower unemployment rates than the workforce of native birth, however, the foreign workforce older than these bands suffered higher unemployment rates.                                 *(229 words)*

### Task 2

Oil, gas and coal are all non-renewable resources. This is known worldwide, as well as the fact that society lives above its demands. Even though fuel prices have increased significantly over the last decade, consumption will still cause these resources to run out eventually. It has been argued that the only way to decrease the usage of fuel is to further increase the prices.

Currently, most people think in the present and do not consider the future enough. Therefore, to affect people in their everyday lives, fuel prices ought to be raised. It is theorised that this will significantly decrease fossil fuel usage, as the economic impact will be forced onto current users. It is necessary that fuel prices are high enough to immediately decrease the wealth of a family and make more people switch to public transport. Critics of this would argue, however, that society's fossil fuels, such as petrol for cars, have an inelastic price and that price hikes would have no effect other than increasing tax and oil company revenues.

In addition, a significant increase in prices would not only impact each individual, but also the whole economy. Fuel prices are not only linked to transport, but also to food production, home heating and entertainment. A rise in prices in all these areas would seriously affect the standard of living of families with limited income and would mean the poorer parts of society would become even poorer.

In conclusion, while raising fuel prices is one of the most commonly-discussed solutions to fuel usage problems, this answer includes too many negative variables. Certainly, increasing fuel prices would create a small reduction of transport usage, but the far-reaching effects would be unfair and unsustainable.                                 *(285 words)*

## ACADEMIC WRITING PRACTICE TEST 4

### Task 1

The bar chart shows the average Australian water consumption in selected cities for last year, while the pie chart shows how water was used in Australia for last year.

It can clearly be seen that water supply affected most of the key parts of Australian life and industry, but the most severely affected sector in a shortage would be agriculture.

The highest water consumer was the city of Perth with 300 kilolitres per property as an annual average. It was followed by Brisbane and Adelaide, where properties used 250 and about 240 kilolitres a year on average. In Sydney, households consumed 200 kilolitres of water annually, and the smallest yearly average consumption was recorded in Melbourne and Canberra, consuming about 150 and 140 kilolitres per property respectively.

Among industries, the largest water user in Australia last year was agriculture, which took up over two thirds of usage at 67%. The next largest usage was by households (9%), water supply, sewage and drainage (7%) and water used for electricity and gas supply (7%). The rest was used by manufacturing (4%), other industries (4%) and mining (2%).                                                (185 words)

### Task 2

Over the last two hundred years, there have been many changes to society in nearly all aspects of people's lives. Medical science has advanced beyond recognition and it can be argued that this has been the most significant change.

The last two centuries have witnessed great advances of the industrial revolution. Automation, machinery and various technologies have revolutionised the way people live, work, play and travel. Society has now many things that make people's lives easier and more enjoyable, including cars, planes, computers and telephones to name only a few. It is quite clear that these advances are phenomenally significant in most people's lives today.

Medical science has also been revolutionised. The three principal challenges facing surgery, which were pain, infection and bleeding, have all been overcome, allowing the lives of millions to be saved. The discoveries of vaccines to deal with the great killer diseases of history also took place over the last two centuries. Probably billions of people who would have died from diseases such as smallpox, tuberculosis, diphtheria and tetanus have all been saved.

In addition to this, medicine now has such an advanced knowledge of human body systems that doctors can cure or heal a wide range of ailments that would in the past have been fatal or extremely debilitating. It is also likely that the next century will see similar significant advances.

In conclusion, although there have been many different advances in society over the last two hundred years, the fact that so many people have had their lives saved or improved by medical breakthroughs makes it seem incontrovertible that it is these medical advances that have been the most significant.
                                                (276 words)

## ACADEMIC WRITING PRACTICE TEST 5

### Task 1

This diagram shows the cycle of pollution that contributes to the development of acid rain and how it affects the environment on which human life is dependent.

The majority of the pollutants created come from housing, transport, factories and power stations. These sources release various compounds such as carbon dioxide, sulphur dioxide, different nitrogen oxides, mercury and other compounds. These pollutants then rise up into the air and are absorbed by clouds, which then become contaminated in turn and travel across countries and continents. Then, once condensation occurs, water containing the pollutants in the clouds will condense and fall to the Earth in the form of precipitation, namely acid rain.

The acid rain will fall onto hills, fields, trees, plants and into rivers and lakes, contaminating them. This leads to the pollution of the environment and the food chain, as the pollutants are absorbed into the Earth or plants, which either act as a habitat or a food source for animals, destroying them or affecting their biological processes. This in turn will lead to the dying out of the animals, which will then lead to imbalance in the food chain, greatly impacting the ecosystem.

(194 words)

### Task 2

Nowadays most information is transmitted over the Internet. A strong dependency on this medium has been created, as personal, political and economic news and information are shared through it. As the Internet is so widely needed, many people believe that governments should provide this access for free. Others believe that Internet access should be paid for.

Before the creation of the Internet, people had phones, newspapers and televisions; nowadays the Internet can replace all of these. Society is now built on a system that relies on everyone having access to the Internet, whether this be in school or in work life. However, while it is seen as a basic necessity in western cultures, the costs for accessing it are still too high for some people. When this point of view is taken into account, it can be concluded that governments should provide access, or a division of inequality will be created in society.

However, when one takes into account the things that the Internet has replaced, it becomes apparent that most of these are not free as well. It is necessary to pay for phone calls, for television and for newspapers. Storing all the information and passing it to consumers through the World Wide Web also entails costs. This raises the question whether the Internet should be handled differently. Providing Internet access to everyone would mean a significant cost for the governments, especially at times of economic crisis. Therefore, this is not a plausible solution to integrate each individual into the society.

In my opinion, while the Internet has become as necessary as a phone, governments should not provide it for free, as the money needed for this would put too much strain on public resources. This finance could be used for even more urgent topics, such as poverty and starvation. *(301 words)*

# COMMENTARY ON THE EXAMPLE SPEAKING RECORDINGS

In this section you will find reports by an IELTS speaking examiner on the recordings of **Speaking Tests 1 - 5**. The questions asked in the recordings are the questions in the Speaking Tests 1 – 5, so, while listening to the recordings, it is advised to have the questions with you for reference. The recordings are not real IELTS test recordings, but the interviewer is a real IELTS examiner and the recordings are conducted in the exact way that an IELTS Speaking Test is done.

## SPEAKING PRACTICE TEST 1

### Examiner's Commentary

The person interviewed is Clara, a French female. Clara is a teacher.

### Part 1

Clara spoke fluently and confidently. She showed that she had an excellent vocabulary range with only very occasional mildly awkward word choices. She showed she could speak at length and on varied topics without needing to pause to access words or grammar, though there were some occasional hesitations. One grammar slip came up when she said "since a long time" rather than 'for a long time.'

### Part 2

Clara spoke well in Part 2. She had no problem with speaking long enough, even though she did not use all the preparation time given. Clara again showed her fluency and accuracy with no pauses and few errors (she said "inconvenient" once instead of 'inconvenience' and she had one missed article). Clara also showed a sense of humour, which is a nice touch in a speaking test. She justified herself well without pausing with the unexpected question at the end.

### Part 3

Again, Clara spoke fluently and accurately and again showed humour. She spoke formally, though occasionally used some informal vocabulary at suitable points. Clara was good at giving full answers, for example, she gave a good list of both advantages and disadvantages of owning a car. In spite of more demanding questions, Clara showed little hesitation and used more complex grammar flexibly and accurately. There were only very occasional errors ("pushing foot down" instead of 'putting' and "consider stop driving" instead of 'consider stopping') and she coped well when searching for a word she didn't know – using "degrees" for alcohol testing, which was perfectly comprehensible.

**Marking** - The marking of the IELTS Speaking Test is done in 4 parts.

| | |
|---|---|
| Fluency and Coherence | 8 |
| Lexical Resource | 8 |
| Grammatical Range and Accuracy | 8 |
| Pronunciation | 8 |
| | |
| **Estimated IELTS Speaking Band** | **8** |

## SPEAKING PRACTICE TEST 2

### Examiner's Commentary

The person interviewed is Darija, a Croatian female. Darija is a personal assistant.

### Part 1

Darija showed that she had a good command of English. Her speech was very clear and there was an American accent apparent. She showed excellent fluency (she got tongue-tied once – not a problem) and gave full answers to all questions. There were no grammar errors and only the very occasional minor awkward word choice.

### Part 2

Darija showed again that her English is fluent, accurate and idiomatic. She had few pauses in her long turn and only occasional fluency trips. There was one grammar error at the end ("than we used to" instead of 'than we are used to').

### Part 3

Darija again showed her excellent command of English with her good and full answers. She was fluent and accurate with only occasional fluency trips and grammar slips ("the nature" instead of 'nature'). Darija's lexical range is excellent, with only the occasional awkward word choice.

**Marking** - The marking of the IELTS Speaking Test is done in 4 parts.

Fluency and Coherence										8
Lexical Resource											8
Grammatical Range and Accuracy							8
Pronunciation											9

**Estimated IELTS Speaking Band**						**8**

**SPEAKING PRACTICE TEST 3**

**Examiner's Commentary**

The person interviewed is Yi Xhuen, a Chinese female. Yi Xhuen is a student.

**Part 1**

Yi Xhuen spoke slowly, but reasonably clearly. She lacked the intonation an English native speaker has and this made her often sound rather wooden. Her pronunciation was fair, but there were some words that were unclear or poorly pronounced (e.g. serious). Yi Xhuen's vocabulary was reasonable, but she lacked range. She was, however, quite good at 'talking round' something and making herself understood when she lacked the words. There were errors though (e.g. "It is over population" instead of 'over-populated'). Yi Xhuen had reasonable grammatical accuracy, but again had a limited range.

**Part 2**

Yi Xhuen took the preparation time available to her, and this is always strongly recommended – there's no advantage to not taking the time. Yi Xhuen was more hesitant with the challenge of the demands of speaking for so long in Part 2 and her fluency was affected. Sometimes she talked herself into a corner and found it difficult to get out. There were also more errors in grammar and word choice. In spite of all this, Yi Xhuen spoke for the required amount of time and made herself understood on different topics and she also showed a sense of humour.

**Part 3**

Yi Xhuen was able to cope with the more demanding questions of Part 3, but her answers could have been longer and more developed. She still showed the intonation, fluency and pronunciation problems of the earlier parts and the more complex topics caused more hesitancy and pauses. She also made more grammar errors, some quite basic ("My country suffer" instead of "My country suffers" – 3rd person agreement). On the other hand, Yi Xhuen spoke for the required amount of time and answered all questions properly and sometimes with examples. Yi Xhuen could certainly always communicate what she wanted to say. Overall, Yi Xhuen's ability in everything was fair, but lacked range and flexibility.

Yi Xhuen's English in Part 3 was much the same as before. She managed to answer each question fully and without too much hesitation, but her grammar and vocabulary ranges were limited and her pronunciation was heavily influenced by her mother tongue. Yi Xhuen has a few limitations in her English, but she can certainly communicate fairly well.

**Marking** - The marking of the IELTS Speaking Test is done in 4 parts.

| | |
|---|---|
| Fluency and Coherence | 5 |
| Lexical Resource | 5 |
| Grammatical Range and Accuracy | 6 |
| Pronunciation | 4 |

**Estimated IELTS Speaking Band**          **5**

## SPEAKING PRACTICE TEST 4

### Examiner's Commentary

The person interviewed is Welta, a Thai female. Welta works in a shop.

### Part 1

Welta addressed all the questions, but there were some problems with all aspects of her English. Her Thai accent was very apparent and this often interfered with communication. For example, the problem with her pronunciation of "r" made her English sound awkward and strange. Some lexis, on the other hand, were pronounced very clearly. Welta had to pause fairly frequently to access ideas and lexis, which affected her fluency. In general, Welta did not give long enough answers. She needed to try and develop most of her answers, so that she could demonstrate a wider range of lexis and grammatical structure. Welta also often misses out words in a sentence, but is confident to carry on, as the words that she does produce usually communicate her meaning.

### Part 2

The problems identified in Part 1 were again apparent. Welta did manage to include some details, however, and managed to talk for over a minute. There were various grammatical and syntactical problems, for example her use of articles. Welta spoke fairly slowly and seemed to lack confidence.

### Part 3

With the added difficulty of Part 3, Welta's performance worsened. The lexis, grammar range and flexibility of thought in English required to deal with the questions were often beyond her English language ability, though she attempted to answer everything. The answers and therefore the entire part were far too short.

**Marking** - The marking of the IELTS Speaking Test is done in 4 parts.

| | |
|---|---|
| Fluency and Coherence | 4 |
| Lexical Resource | 4 |
| Grammatical Range and Accuracy | 4 |
| Pronunciation | 4 |

**Estimated IELTS Speaking Band       4**

## SPEAKING PRACTICE TEST 5

### Examiner's Commentary

The person interviewed is Eva, a Latvian female. Eva is a teacher.

### Part 1

Eva spoke fluently and accurately in this Part. She has an accent, but it does not obstruct communication. Eva has a very good vocabulary range and accurate grammar usage. There was one error (i.e. "from Internet" instead of 'from the Internet'), but it was extremely minor. She provided good full answers and only paused to think about good answers for questions.

### Part 2

Eva did not need the preparation time, which was available. She performed fine, but I would not recommend not using the time given. Eva was fluent and accurate and used a very good and natural vocabulary range. The accent was still apparent, but did not hinder understanding. Eva did not make any grammar errors.

### Part 3

Eva again showed excellent fluency, grammar and vocabulary range. The accent is still there, but again it does not stop communication or understanding.

**Marking** - The marking of the IELTS Speaking Test is done in 4 parts.

| | |
|---|---|
| Fluency and Coherence | 8 |
| Lexical Resource | 8 |
| Grammatical Range and Accuracy | 8 |
| Pronunciation | 7 |

**Estimated IELTS Speaking Band**    **8**

# Listening Recordings' Transcripts

## LISTENING TEST 1 TRANSCRIPT

**This recording is copyright by Robert Nicholson and Simone Braverman, all rights reserved.**

**IELTS listening practice tests. Test one. In the IELTS test you hear some recordings and you have to answer questions on them. You have time to read the instructions and questions and check your work. All recordings are played only once. The test is in four parts. Now turn to part one.**

**Part one. You will hear a conversation between a man and a woman discussing lost property at a cinema.**

**First you have some time to look at questions one to five.**

*(20 second gap)*

**Now we begin. You should answer the questions as you listen, as the recording is not played twice. Listen carefully to the conversation and answer questions one to five.**

| | |
|---|---|
| Peter | Good morning. Do you work here at this cinema? |
| Angela | Yes, I do. My name's Angela. Can I help you? |
| Peter | I was here last night watching a film and I think I dropped my wallet under my seat. |
| Angela | Oh, I don't have the keys for the lost property drawer. I can take some information for you and I'll get Mr. Smith to call you when he comes in. He's in charge of lost property. |
| Peter | That'll be fine. |
| Angela | What's your name? |
| Peter | Peter Simpson. Simpson is spelled S - I - M - P - S - O – N **(Q1)**. |
| Angela | And can you let me know your address? |
| Peter | I live at thirteen **(Q2)**. Winchester Road, Alton. |
| Angela | And the postcode? |
| Peter | It's W twelve, seven RT. **(Q3)** |
| Angela | Now, I need a contact telephone number for you. |
| Peter | I'll give you my mobile number, as that'll be more convenient. It's oh one seven four three, oh six two, four nine six. |
| Angela | Thanks. Now, what film were you watching? |
| Peter | It was the new Spiderman movie. |

Page 153

| | |
|---|---|
| Angela | What showing did you see? |
| Peter | It was the one that began at <u>seven-thirty p.m</u>. **(Q4)**. |
| Angela | Do you remember where you were sitting? |
| Peter | Yes. I still have my ticket. Here it is. I was in seat <u>F twenty-three</u> **(Q5)**. There was only one other person near me in G twenty-four, so my wallet shouldn't have been found by another customer. |
| Angela | Thanks. |

**Before the conversation continues, you have some time to look at questions six to ten.**

*(20 second gap)*

**Now listen carefully and answer questions six to ten.**

| | |
|---|---|
| Angela | Now, could you give me some details about the contents of your wallet? |
| Peter | Well, I had <u>some cash, around twenty pounds I think</u> **(Q6-Q10)**. Then there were my bank cards, <u>my debit card, and credit cards</u> **(Q6-Q10)**. |
| Angela | Have you cancelled them yet? |
| Peter | Yes, I did that this morning when I realised that my wallet was missing. I don't keep a note of the PIN numbers in my wallet, so the cards should be safe. |
| Angela | Anything else? |
| Peter | <u>My company ID is in there</u> **(Q6-Q10)**. That's a card that I swipe when I go into work. I usually have my company photocopy card in there as well, but for some reason I left that on my desk. |
| Angela | OK. I've made a note of that. |
| Peter | Next week, <u>I'm coming back to the cinema for another film. I bought the ticket last night, so that is in the wallet too</u> **(Q6-Q10)**. I'm also going to the theatre, but that ticket is in the glove compartment of my car. |
| Angela | Anything else? We've had people who lost wallets with hotel card keys, library cards, health insurance cards, passports and lots of other things. |
| Peter | Yes, you're right. <u>I do have my health insurance card in there</u> **(Q6-Q10)**. I'd forgotten. But that's it. |
| Angela | Right then. Thanks very much, Mr. Simpson. I'm sorry I can't tell you more right now, but I'll give this information to Mr. Smith the moment he gets in and I'll make sure he calls right away. |
| Peter | Thanks very much. Goodbye. |
| Angela | Goodbye. |

Page 154

**That is the end of part one. You will now have half a minute to check your answers.**

*(30 second gap)*

**Now turn to part two.**

**Part two. You will hear a woman telling some people about the organisation of a conference. First you have some time to look at questions eleven to fifteen.**

*(20 second gap)*

**Now listen carefully to the information talk and answer questions eleven to fifteen.**

Good morning and welcome to this first talk of the conference on the conservation of natural resources. My name is Linda. Before we start with our first official speaker, I'd like to tell you a little about the organisation of the event.

First of all, I'd like to tell you that within the conference areas, all your food and non-alcoholic drinks are free, as the costs have been included within the price of your ticket. All you need to do is to show the blue identification card that you were issued when you registered. If you wear it round your neck with the string provided, then it is easily seen and not easy to lose. If you do lose it, please come to see me at my catering desk with some identification and I'll issue you a new one. As you came into the conference area earlier through the main entrance, you will have seen a large rectangular room, which is the conference reception room. The catering desk is in this room, just to the right of the conference entrance as you come in **(Q11)**. If you have not yet officially registered, you can do that at the registration desk across the room directly opposite my catering desk **(Q12)**. Again, just bring a piece of identification.

We know that some of you will not have yet organised anywhere to stay. If you'd like some help with that, you can visit our accommodation desk, which is found to the left of the registration desk as you come into the conference reception room **(Q13)**. The bathrooms are between these two desks. We have agreed some special rates at some nearby hotels that also have free shuttle services to and from this conference centre. You won't find a better deal.

During the conference, there will be two speeches going on at any one time. After the opening speech that follows my talk, you can choose to stay in this hall, which is Lancaster Hall, or go to the other hall, which is Kensington Hall. Lancaster Hall, which is the one we are in right now, is through the only door in the right hand wall of the conference reception room **(Q14)** and Kensington Hall is directly opposite **(Q15)**. Plans and schedules are available on the desk on the left of the conference reception room entrance as you come in. Please help yourself.

**You now have some time to look at questions sixteen to twenty.**

*(20 second gap)*

**Now listen to the rest of the information talk and answer questions sixteen to twenty.**

And now, before the opening speech, I'd like to tell you about the refreshments organised for this event.

In the mornings before the first speeches, we will have tea, coffee, juices and water along with <u>some fruit</u> **(Q16)** available on tables. Please help yourselves, but please don't take food or drinks into the conference halls. Just leave used crockery on the tables provided.

Lunches will be served in the conference centre's restaurant. To get there, leave our conference area and go up to <u>the second floor</u> **(Q17)** by lift, escalator or stairs. You will see the restaurant there easily. In the restaurant, the food will be served cafeteria style, so that the large number of people can be handled efficiently. There will be starters, soups and salads available as well as main courses. The main course will have two meat options, one vegetarian option and <u>one</u> **(Q18)** vegan option. There will be the usual side dishes such as potatoes, pasta, rice and a range of vegetables. There will also be a choice of deserts and fruit to finish your meal. Drinks are also available in the restaurant. As I said before, everything soft will be free of charge, but you will have to pay extra for things like wine and beer. Tea and coffee will be available in the restaurant as well.

In the afternoon, we will serve tea in the conference area. However, if the weather is good, we will serve the tea <u>on the terrace</u> **(Q19)**. Tea, coffee, juices and water will be available to drink and to eat there will be a selection of sandwiches, cakes and biscuits. These will be laid out for you, so just help yourselves.

If you have any queries or complaints, please come and see me. In the morning and afternoons, I will be at the catering desk and at lunchtimes, I will be stationed <u>in the restaurant</u> **(Q20)**.

I'll stop now and hand you over to our first official speaker.

**That is the end of part two. You will now have half a minute to check your answers.**

*(30 second gap)*

**Now turn to part three.**

**Part three. You will hear a student and a lecturer discussing a university course on coastal erosion. First you have some time to look at questions twenty-one to twenty-five.**

*(20 second gap)*

**Now listen carefully and answer questions twenty-one to twenty-five.**

| Amanda | Good morning, Dr. Peters. Can I ask you a couple of questions? |
| --- | --- |
| Dr. Peters | Oh, good morning, Amanda. Yes, I'm free right now. Go ahead. |
| Amanda | I wanted to ask you about the course that you're offering next year on coastal erosion. |
| Dr. Peters | OK. |
| Amanda | First, I wanted to know which country the course focuses on. |

Dr. Peters      Well, I don't restrict myself. As we're in Australia, it's natural that I spend quite a bit of the course focusing on the coastline here. Australia has a coastline of nearly thirty-six thousand kilometres and around fifty per cent **(Q21)** of that is made up of sand. Australia provides us with so much material to work on and is currently such a topical subject that we don't need to study anywhere else. That would make the course a little limited though and so we look at various other places around the world.

Amanda      What are some of the other locations?

Dr. Peters      There are some cliff formations **(Q22)** in California that are in danger from the Pacific there, so we look at that. A lot of the countries in Western Africa have erosion problems and this is quite an important part of the course.

Amanda      Is it true that the West African erosion problem is because of human activities?

Dr. Peters      It's simplistic to blame problems on only one cause, but human actions are certainly part of the problem. The removal of sand and gravel from the coast to use for construction and human coastal constructions, such as ports, harbours and jetties, with the associated dredging required for ships to approach, have all exacerbated the problems. Natural phenomena, such as wave actions, tide, sea currents and winds also play a role, although it's argued global warming **(Q23)** affects these as well.

Amanda      Are there any other places we study?

Dr. Peters      We look at some severe erosion areas around the world, so we can study the causes, consequences and action taken in these areas. This includes some locations in the UK, Louisiana and Hawaii. There are various others as well.

Amanda      Do we have many field trips?

Dr. Peters      Yes, we do, but only in Australia and to places not too far away. We can't afford to go to Africa and California unfortunately! Our main trip is a study of the Gold Coast and we visit a number of hotspots **(Q24)** on the coast there.

Amanda      What will we do on the field trips?

Dr. Peters       A lot of survey work and research. Fortunately, we have the figures of previous students available, so we have great data on past erosion measurements. You'll have access to all these data and then you'll need to do your own measurements.

Amanda      How long will the trips be?

Dr. Peters      They'll be mostly day trips when possible to keep costs down. That will of course be locations that are fairly close to us here. There will also have to be some overnight **(Q25)** trips. We get a lot of work done on these trips, but it's a lot of fun as well.

**You now have some time to look at questions twenty-six to thirty.**

*(20 second gap)*

**Now listen to the rest of the discussion and answer questions twenty-six to thirty.**

Amanda      Can I ask you a little about assessment?

Dr. Peters      Yes, of course. The assessment is divided between essays, a project and one exam at the end of the academic year.

Amanda      What does each of those entail?

Dr. Peters      You'll have six essays. These will be set on different areas of the course and they will try to make you look more deeply at different geographical locations and at the different causes and consequences **(Q26)** of the problems and actions taken or planned. The project is for you to choose an area of study that has interested you. As we're in Australia, it's natural that most students choose an erosion issue or situation here, as information is more readily available and the locations are easier to visit. We do have students who choose overseas locations, particularly foreign students **(Q27)**, of course.

Amanda      And the exam?

Dr. Peters      The exam is two hours **(Q28)** in length and will assess the whole course. Any part of the course can come up and students will be expected to have a good working knowledge of the various aspects of the different things that they studied.

Amanda      How are the assessments weighted?

Dr. Peters      The exam is fifteen per cent of the final course grade and the essays are thirty-five per cent. The project makes up the other fifty per cent.

Amanda      What happens if students fail?

Dr. Peters      The exam **(Q29)** can be re-taken if the students fail, but the essays and project cannot be done again. It's not that easy a course. There is a lot of knowledge to acquire and synthesise.

Amanda      Do you get many students who fail?

Dr. Peters      No, not really. The key thing for us is the student selection. We try and make sure that we choose able and motivated students. We check qualifications very carefully to ensure that all students have the necessary background and skills to cope with what the course demands.

Amanda      That sounds reassuring.

Dr. Peters      I hope so. Of course there are occasionally some problems, but usually, the course tutors **(Q30)** can see fairly early by the essay performances if any students are struggling and they try to intervene and help before the problem students' situations become irretrievable.

Amanda      Well, thanks, Dr. Peters. That was really helpful!

Dr. Peters      You're welcome, Amanda. Goodbye.

Amanda      Goodbye.

**That is the end of part three. You will now have half a minute to check your answers.**

*(30 second gap)*

**Now turn to part four.**

**Part four. You will hear part of a biology lecture on the emperor penguin. First you have some time to look at questions thirty-one to forty.**

*(50 second gap)*

**Now listen carefully and answer questions thirty-one to forty.**

Good morning and welcome to this lecture on the emperor penguin. Penguins in general are flightless birds perfectly designed for the marine environment. They are excellent swimmers with a torpedo shaped body, feet and tail that act as a rudder and flippers that act as propellers. A waterproof coat of feathers with an under-layer of woolly down plus a <u>fat **(Q31)**</u> layer protects them against the cold.

Penguins eat mainly small fish and krill. In turn, penguins become food for other marine animals, namely leopard seals and <u>killer whales **(Q32)**</u>. On land, their main predators are skuas and sheathbills, which are both carnivorous birds that take both eggs and chicks.

There is still debate about the classification of some penguins, and depending on which authority is followed, there are seventeen, and perhaps up to twenty, species of penguin. Four of these species live and nest on and around the Antarctic continent and the rest are found in sub-Antarctic regions.

The largest of the penguin species, the emperor grows up to 1.15 metres tall and weighs up to forty kilograms. They are very deep divers, often diving to about two hundred and fifty metres with dives lasting on average three to six minutes. Their menu is varied and includes fish, krill and squid.

A truly hardy animal, the emperor penguin is the only warm-blooded animal that breeds during the Antarctic winter, surviving blizzards, darkness and wind chill equivalent to temperatures as low as minus sixty degrees Celsius. Every year around late March, adult emperor penguins leave the pack ice and may walk up to two hundred kilometres over its frozen surface to their breeding sites. <u>They require stable, long-lasting fast ice **(Q33)**</u> on which to breed. In May or June, the females lay one egg and then make the long walk back to open water, eating again for the first time in about two months. In the meantime, <u>the egg is kept on the feet of the father, protected under the layers of feathers and fat of its abdomen **(Q34)**</u>. During the next two months, the father fasts while keeping watch until its chick hatches. Miraculously, at that time, the mother returns with food. By that time of year, July - August, food can then be obtained more easily, because adjacent ocean areas have been swept free of sea ice by strong winds.

Two of the most northern emperor penguin populations are located at Pointe Géologie, Adélie Land, and Dion Island located on the northwestern Antarctic Peninsula. In this warmer part of Antarctica, both emperor penguin populations have declined over recent decades. <u>At Pointe Géologie, the population has declined by about fifty per cent over the past fifty years. High mortality occurred during the late 1970's, the cause of which is not yet known, and the population has not recovered since **(Q35)**</u>. The decrease in the Dion Island colony was brought about by large-scale disappearance of sea ice in that region.

The emperor penguins' main predator is the leopard seal. The leopard seal lives in the ocean and waits until some emperor penguins enter the water and then eats the weakest one. Also some birds eat the eggs and the chicks when they are about a month old. Furthermore, emperor penguins face threats from overfishing and rising temperatures. The overfishing **(Q36)** is killing most of the emperor penguins' food source.

Climate change has caused profound changes in the Antarctic ecosystem and impacts the emperor penguins in diverse ways, such as causing ice shelves to collapse and icebergs to calve. A recent report claims that under two degrees Celsius **(Q37)** global warming will lead to a decrease in sea ice thickness and an increase in open water area. This will severely challenge around forty percent of the emperor penguin population in terms of finding satisfactory nesting areas **(Q38)**. The report goes on to say that because of this, emperor penguins will lose twenty per cent of their number in the next ten years; the report also calls for emperor penguins to be put on the endangered animals list. Global warming can paradoxically cause more and less ice at different times of year. Too much ice can mean that the female has much further to travel to begin to feed following the birth and much further therefore to return to bring the food to the hatched chick and waiting father. Too little ice can mean that breeding platforms **(Q39)** can be scarcer or break up earlier before the chicks are ready. The report hopes that emperor penguins may adapt to the changing conditions, by climbing onto land or higher, safer ice, but at this point, this is only conjecture.

A final threat is that the king penguin may also easily displace the emperor penguin because of its extended breeding season, which allows it to exist in areas with lower food **(Q40)** availability.

**That is the end of part four. You will now have half a minute to check your answers.**

*(30 second gap)*

**That is the end of listening test one.**

## LISTENING TEST 2 TRANSCRIPT

**This recording is copyright by Robert Nicholson and Simone Braverman, all rights reserved.**

**IELTS listening practice tests. Test two. In the IELTS test you hear some recordings and you have to answer questions on them. You have time to read the instructions and questions and check your work. All recordings are played only once. The test is in four parts. Now turn to part one.**

**Part one. You will hear a conversation between a man and a woman discussing a celebration at an outdoor centre.**

**First you have some time to look at questions one to five.**

*(20 second gap)*

**Now we begin. You should answer the questions as you listen, as the recording is not played twice. Listen carefully to the conversation and answer questions one to five.**

John        Good morning. Welcome to John's Outdoor Centre.

Katherine        Thank you.

John        What can I do for you?

Katherine        I'm looking for a suitable place to celebrate my birthday. When I drove by this place a couple of days ago, I thought that this might be a good place, as it is quite far from the city. It would be a really different place to be.

John        May I ask when your birthday is?

Katherine        On the eighteenth of <u>May</u> **(Q1)**.

John        Alright. In the summer. That's a very nice time. We would be able to use the stone oven, make a bonfire and use the camping area if you wish to stay for the night.

Katherine        That sounds great!

John        OK. May I first take your phone number and full name before we start to talk about any further details?

Katherine        Of course! My full name is Katherine Truman – that's spelt K - A - T - H - E - R - I - N - E and <u>T - R - U - M - A - N</u> **(Q2)**. And my telephone number is oh three four eight, two three seven, eight five five.

John        Got that, thank you. So, when's the party supposed to be?

Katherine        I'd like to celebrate on the twentieth of May and the party should start at <u>6 p.m.</u> **(Q3)**, because I still need to work on that day and then get ready for the party, which I guess you know will take some time!

Page 161

John        Oh dear, working on a Saturday. I know nobody who enjoys that! Well, my calendar shows that the date is free and, up to now, there haven't been any other bookings made for that day yet. However, horse riding (Q4) is not available on that day, as the horses will be resting. I hope that you didn't plan to do that?

Katherine   Oh no, that's fine. I think that food and a bonfire will be fine for my guests.

John        Speaking of guests. How many people have you invited or are you intending to invite?

Katherine   It'll be thirty people (Q5).

John        Okay.

**Before the conversation continues, you have some time to look at questions six to ten.**

*(20 second gap)*

**Now listen carefully and answer questions six to ten.**

Katherine   Before I book any activities for the party, I would like to have a list of the activities that are available and their prices. My budget is eight hundred dollars and I would like to stay within this boundary. This must also include the food and drinks consumed.

John        Okay. Let's go through the price lists. So, as you can see, we are open from seven a.m. to eight p.m. from Monday through Friday. On the weekends, however, we are open from eight-thirty a.m. to seven p.m (Q6). These opening times don't interfere with your party, as you're planning to spend the night here, aren't you?

Katherine   It depends on the price I would have to pay.

John        Okay, so we offer various activities. To start with, we can offer to make a bonfire for fifteen dollars. This money is just to pay for the wood we need.

Katherine   Yeah, that sounds great. I'll definitely book the bonfire. What else is there?

John        There are also various tours we offer, like for instance the boat tour, which takes between two and three hours and costs six dollars (Q7) per person. Then there is the cycling tour for eight dollars per person and the hiking tour for twenty-five dollars per person. Our special offer for the summer is baking in our newly built stone oven. This can be done in groups of up to fifteen people maximum and costs five dollars (Q8) per person.

Katherine   Okay, that sounds great. Let me see. I would really like to bake, so I'll take that. And I'll also take the boat tour.

John          Alright. Let's get to the food and drinks. We offer a small and a large buffet. The small one serves approximately forty people and costs two hundred dollars, while the large one costs <u>four hundred dollars</u> **(Q9)** and serves eighty to a hundred people. As an extra, you can also book a lamb on a spit for thirty-five dollars. I think for you, I'd plan one hundred and fifty dollars for the drinks.

Katherine     Alright, then I'll take the small buffet please and the drinks of course.

John          Okay, and lastly we offer three types of accommodation. We can offer camping with tents for forty dollars per tent and they hold four people each. We also have some tipis, which are big tents that hold up to twenty people, for eighty dollars per tipi. However, our greatest attraction is the tree house for <u>a hundred dollars</u> **(Q10)**. It can house up to twenty people as well.

Katherine     Okay. Half of my guests will drive back home, so the tree house will be perfect. Great! According to my calculations that makes seven hundred and ninety-five dollars in total, so that's just under my budget.

John          Yes, I think that's right.

Katherine     Okay. Thank you for that. Could we take a look at the tree house?

John          Of course we can. It's right over there.

**That is the end of part one. You will now have half a minute to check your answers.**

*(30 second gap)*

**Now turn to part two.**

**Part two. You will hear a woman giving some people information about a walking tour around the town of Barton. First you have some time to look at questions eleven to fourteen.**

*(20 second gap)*

**Now listen carefully to the information talk and answer questions eleven to fourteen.**

Good morning, everyone. My name's Sharon. Thanks for coming today to my walking tour of the town of Barton. First, I'd like to give you a quick overview of where we're going to today.

Right now, we're in front of the Barton Tourist Office. From here, we'll move down the pedestrian road towards the river. While we're on this road, <u>we'll first pass the Town Hall on the right and then right after that, the old town prison. Opposite the prison we'll see the town museum</u> **(Q11)**, although we won't be visiting that this morning. When we get to the river, you'll see the river docks, where people can take boat trips up and down the River Stroud. We'll turn right here and walk down the path next to the river. While we're walking, we'll first see on the right the Museum of Modern Art and then after that, the oldest house in the town and then, just before we get to Charlton Bridge, the memorial to Sir John Barton, the founder of the town. <u>Across the river from the Modern Art Museum, we'll see the impressive facade of the main town mosque</u> **(Q12)**, which was built only fifteen years ago for the Muslim population of the town.

Page 163

We won't cross Charlton Bridge, but we'll go to the right again and walk up the street, stopping at Regent Square, in the centre of which is the town's war memorial fountain **(Q13)**. There's a great ice cream parlour there and we can rest a while, look at the view and eat some ice cream. When we're done with that, we'll take the road that goes right off the square and walk back down towards the Tourist Office again. While we're walking, you'll see Barton Shopping Mall on the right **(Q14).** We won't stop there on our tour, but if you want to do some shopping, it's only a short walk back. There are a number of interesting things to see on the left. You'll first see the town's famous gothic church and then the library and sports centre. For your information, the town's train station is right behind the library as we pass it and the cinema is next to that.

**You now have some time to look at questions fifteen to twenty.**

*(20 second gap)*

**Now listen to the rest of the information talk and answer questions fifteen to twenty.**

I'll be speaking at each of the attractions to let you know all the interesting information, so I think the tour will take around two and a half hours **(Q15)** and that's including the twenty-minute break for ice cream. This afternoon, I'll be doing a three-hour walking tour of the town museum that we will pass early on in this walk.

By the way, I do not charge anything for this walk **(Q16)** and I live only by tips. If you feel the walk has been worthwhile, past walkers with me have tipped between five and twenty pounds. It depends on your budget and how good a job you think I've done.

Now, just before we begin, I've been asked to talk a little bit about the entertainment on offer tonight around the town.

Tonight is a weekday, so there's not much in the way of live music, which someone asked me about. Nor will you find here much in the way of football, as the town team only plays at the weekends. At the town cinema, there is a double bill film with films on novels by the famous Russian novelist **(Q17-Q20)**, Leo Tolstoy. That starts at seven o'clock. We won't see the town theatre on our walk today, but there is a tour of it offered tonight as there are no performances tonight **(Q17-Q20).** You might be tired of tours today by then though!

One fun thing to do that does not involve any walking is at the pub called The Crown. They have their weekly quiz on tonight **(Q17-Q20).** I often go to that myself with some friends. What I will be doing tonight though is to go to a cafe in the town's main square, where I will be watching some street theatre **(Q17-Q20)** that is scheduled this evening to start at eight o'clock. Barton is quite well known for this, so it would be an excellent and different thing to do. There is some tennis on in London too and I told some people that they could watch that on TV in their hotel or in pubs, but I've been told that bad weather in London has stopped all play, so that won't be an option any more.

So, those are a few things you could consider and maybe I'll see you later if you do what I'm doing. Now, let's get on with our walking tour!

**That is the end of part two. You will now have half a minute to check your answers.**

*(30 second gap)*

**Now turn to part three.**

**Part three. You will hear three students and a lecturer discussing the students' agriculture projects. First you have some time to look at questions twenty-one to twenty-five.**

*(20 second gap)*

**Now listen carefully and answer questions twenty-one to twenty-five.**

Professor Evans       Now, you three have come to tell me how you're getting on with your agriculture projects.

Simona       That's right, Professor Evans.

Professor Evans:       So, to start with, I'd like to you to tell me about the collection of your primary data. Would you like to start, Steve?

Steve       Of course. I've been studying how parasites affect the growing of potatoes in this part of the world. In order to gather data, I've liaised with some farmers **(Q21)** local to the university and they've nearly all allowed me to work in their fields and collect data. The problem is that all the farmers around here use insecticides that kill the parasites. It's been easy therefore to collect information on farms with no parasite dangers, but it was a challenge to get information on farms that had parasites.

Professor Evans       How did you manage to get the parasite data then?

Steve       I had to rent a field **(Q22)** away from other farms and plant potatoes myself. I of course did not use insecticides and I've managed to collect enough data to compare with the other data on farms with insecticides.

Robert       Wasn't that expensive, Steve?

Steve       Not too bad actually. There was an initial outlay for the rental and the planting, but I managed to do a deal with a local farmer, who harvested and sold them. He paid me for them and, as they were bio-potatoes with no insecticides, I got a good price and I even made a small profit. My housemates and I also ate potatoes every day for a couple of weeks!

Professor Evans       How about you, Simona?

Simona       Well, as you know, I'm doing a project on growth rates **(Q23)** in different varieties of tomatoes. Now the weather here is not so good for tomatoes, but the university botanical garden assigned me an area in one of their greenhouses and so I was able to grow plenty of varieties and I had lots of success with gathering data for my project. Like Steve, my house ate lots of tomatoes through the early summer!

Professor Evans       So, Robert. How did you get on?

Robert          I had a lot of initial problems. I wanted to look at different soils and how acidity **(Q24)** affected growth of certain plants. I started a bit too late and I wasn't able to get agreements with different places about being able to use the different bits of land with the acidities that I wanted.

Professor Evans          How did you deal with that?

Robert          In the end, I just had to ditch that idea and go for my plan B. This was about the growing techniques of apple farmers. The season **(Q25)** starts later, so I had enough time to prepare and contact farmers. Where I live at home with my parents is an important apple-growing area, so I was able to use my holidays to gather all the information there.

**You now have some time to look at questions twenty-six to thirty.**

*(20 second gap)*

**Now listen to the rest of the discussion and answer questions twenty-six to thirty.**

Professor Evans the project?          So, do you have any questions about the rest of the work that you need to do on

Steve different things.          We're a little confused about when we need to be finished by. We've heard

Professor Evans          You need to give me a hard copy **(Q26)** by the twenty-eighth of February next year. I then have a week to read your projects and make comments on what you need to do to improve. You then have until the thirtieth of April **(Q27)** to submit the final version to the university. Remember as well that you can't give in a hard copy this year. It has to be submitted by email to the course administrator, which is Mrs. Roberts. Her email address is in the course literature, on our website and on the department noticeboard.

Simona          There is no mention in the project guide about a word limit. Is there one?

Professor Evans          Yes, there is. It's in the project guide, but it's hard to find. We'll make it clearer next year. Last year, the word limit was deemed insufficient at eight thousand words, so this year it's been increased by two thousand **(Q28)**. We hope that this will give you all the scope to do a good job. Be careful not to waffle though or we'll be cutting it down by a thousand next year for those after you. The limit also doesn't include the appendices **(Q29)**, which is another change from last year. There's no limit on them, but please be sensible and don't give me twenty thousand words!

Robert          I've a last question, Professor. What happens if our projects are not good enough?

Professor Evans          That doesn't happen very often, Robert. I'll get to read the first drafts and, unless the project is incredibly bad, I can give you the advice needed to get it up to scratch. If in the end it really does fail, then you won't be able to graduate **(Q30)**. You'd have to redo the project or do a different one the next year in your own time.

Robert          Thanks, Professor.

**That is the end of part three. You will now have half a minute to check your answers.**

*(30 second gap)*

**Now turn to part four.**

**Part four. You will hear part of a psychology lecture on the Rorschach Test. First you have some time to look at questions thirty-one to forty.**

*(50 second gap)*

**Now listen carefully and answer questions thirty-one to forty.**

Good afternoon, everyone. Today, we continue our overview of the different psychological tests that have been used over the years in order to profile people and to explain out-of-the ordinary behaviour. The test we'll look at today is the Rorschach Test.

The Rorschach Test is a projective psychological test developed in nineteen twenty-one to measure thought disorder. It was first developed from the observation that schizophrenia patients often interpret ambiguous images in very unusual ways **(Q31)**. In the test, a participant is shown a series of ten ink blot cards and is directed to respond to each by saying what the ink blots look like. The Rorschach Test is practically the only test that evaluates in this way **(Q32)**.

The Rorschach ink blots are supposed to remain secret so as not to pollute the test population **(Q33)**. The theory behind the test, created by Hermann Rorschach, is that a test taker's spontaneous or unrehearsed responses reveal deep secrets or significant information about his or her personality or innermost thoughts. These days, nearly all psychologists avoid using the method applied to the Rorschach, as it is regarded as unreliable at best and dangerously misleading at worst **(Q34)**. A few psychologists, however, still believe in it as a valid diagnostic tool, despite the availability of more modern and sophisticated personality tests. The psychologists who do still see value in the Rorschach Test frequently argue amongst themselves as to the manner of its interpretation, the meaning of the results, and even its validity **(Q35)**. Several different schools of thought have even sprung up for the interpretation of the results, muddying the waters even further.

For those still using the Rorschach Test, the Exner Comprehensive System is one of the more popular scoring methodologies in use today. Based on the work of John E. Exner, responses are scored using a number of categories. There is a reference to the level of vagueness of the answer or if there is a synthesis of multiple images in the blot. What makes a subject say what he or she does is also significant. For example, how the respondents explain how the ink blots resemble what they think it resembles is very significant. Amongst other criteria, the degree of mental organising activity that is involved in producing the response and any illogical, incongruous, or incoherent aspects of responses are also used in evaluation. Using the scores for these categories, the examiner then performs a series of mathematical calculations producing a structural summary of the test data. The results of the structural summary are claimed to show personality characteristics **(Q36)** that have been demonstrated to be related to different kinds of responses. Both the calculations of scores and the interpretation are often done electronically.

The Rorschach Test is supposed to be administered in a very particular and rigid format in order to minimise variance **(Q37)** in the results. Like the cards themselves, the test procedure itself is also supposed to be kept secret from the general public. In the standard test protocol, test takers are given the cards one at a time in a specific order, and the psychologist is supposed to place them directly in the takers' hands facing up and in a particular orientation. The order is not supposed to vary. The genuine Rorschach cards are numbered on the back primarily for the psychologists' use. If takers notice the numbers or remark on them, a note is supposed to be made about this. The cards themselves are large, about seven by nine inches and are made of stiffened cardboard or, in modern variations, a textured plastic that mimics the feel of cardboard. Five of the cards have purely black and white images, two of the cards are black, white, and red, and the last three cards have various colours of ink used in the blots.

The test giver will almost never give any guidance **(Q38)**. They will instead tell the test takers that they're free to do whatever they like with the card. About fifty per cent of people who take the test flip or rotate the cards. It's reported that some psychologists will penalise people in terms of the results if they don't turn the cards around or upside-down!

During the test the psychologist or psychiatrist will record everything the taker says. In general, questioning or asking about the results are supposed to have significance to the test provider, as does asking nearly anything about the blots themselves. It used to be that the notes were taken in a special shorthand **(Q39)** that was specifically developed for the Rorschach Test, although these days many psychologists rely more on recordings and will only make cursory hand-written notes during the test. Often the psychologist will attempt to shield his or her note-taking from the takers so as not to distract them or make them nervous **(Q40)**, as this would create a skew in the test results.

**That is the end of part four. You will now have half a minute to check your answers.**

*(30 second gap)*

**That is the end of listening test two.**

## LISTENING TEST 3 TRANSCRIPT

**This recording is copyright by Robert Nicholson and Simone Braverman, all rights reserved.**

**IELTS listening practice tests. Test three. In the IELTS test you hear some recordings and you have to answer questions on them. You have time to read the instructions and questions and check your work. All recordings are played only once. The test is in four parts. Now turn to part one.**

**Part one. You will hear a conversation between a man and a woman discussing a mobile phone contract.**

**First you have some time to look at questions one to five.**

*(20 second gap)*

**Now we begin. You should answer the questions as you listen, as the recording is not played twice. Listen carefully to the conversation and answer questions one to five.**

| Tom | Hello. Welcome to R and N Mobile. My name's Tom. How can I help you? |
|---|---|
| Jennifer | Hello. I'd like to discuss my new mobile contract. |
| Tom | Would you mind giving me your customer ID? |
| Jennifer | Just a moment, please. Here it is. TR three four nine five seven three. |
| Tom | Thank you. Now, just for confirmation, could you provide me with your date of birth? |
| Jennifer | Sure. It's the twelfth of March, <u>nineteen eighty-two</u> **(Q1)**. |
| Tom | And what's the zip code of your current address? |
| Jennifer | It's eight five eight two three. |
| Tom | What's the number of your house at that location? |
| Jennifer | <u>Thirty</u> **(Q2)**. |
| Tom | And finally, your name, please? |
| Jennifer | Jennifer Wright. |
| Tom | Would you spell that, please? |
| Jennifer | Jennifer is J - E - double N - I - F - E - R. Wright is <u>W - R - I - G - H - T</u> **(Q3)**. |

Tom    That's interesting. We had you before as Jennifer with only one N. I'll just change that. Now, I notice here that we don't have a home number for you. That can be very useful for us in case you have a problem on your mobile and we can't phone you on it.

| Jennifer | My home number is oh one nine three four, <u>nine eight one</u> **(Q4)**, three four two. |
| --- | --- |
| Tom | Finally, can you just confirm for me how you pay your monthly bill? |
| Jennifer | I do that with <u>direct debit</u> **(Q5)**. |
| Tom | OK, Miss Wright. Thank you. That has confirmed your identity. |

**Before the conversation continues, you have some time to look at questions six to ten.**

*(20 second gap)*

**Now listen carefully and answer questions six to ten.**

| Jennifer | Last Wednesday, I ordered a new contract, but I only saw yesterday that the terms have changed. |
| --- | --- |
| Tom | Absolutely right. |
| Jennifer | Now, I wanted to know whether I am also eligible to have an additional <u>two gigabytes</u> **(Q6)** of Internet each month. |
| Tom | Just a moment, please. (*pause*) OK. I just looked into this, and I'm sorry to say that you're not eligible. |
| Jennifer | Could you do anything about it? |
| Tom | As a matter of fact, you are in luck. As you did not yet activate the <u>SIM card</u> **(Q7)**, we will be able to send you a new contract along with a new SIM card. |
| Jennifer | That would be great. Are there any extra costs? |
| Tom | No, there will be no extra costs for you. Furthermore, you will also be able to use our TFR Network, which is one of the fastest available. |
| Jennifer | That sounds great. And how about the terms and conditions? Will I be able to terminate the contract? |
| Tom | Absolutely. You'll be able to terminate the contract, but you must, however, terminate <u>thirty</u> **(Q8)** days in advance. |
| Jennifer | Sounds great. And the price of <u>forty-five</u> **(Q9)** dollars per month will stay the same? |
| Tom | Exactly. May I proceed to delete your current contract and start the new one? |
| Jennifer | Absolutely. Could I also order a new mobile telephone? |
| Tom | Yes, you will be able to do that on our website. I will send you an email with the <u>link</u> **(Q10)** to our online store. I have now also changed your contract. You'll be able to reauthorise your payment, so you'll just need to sign here, please. That's it. Can I help you in any other way? |

**Page 170**

| | |
|---|---|
| Jennifer | No, that's all. Thank you very much. |
| Tom | You're welcome. Have a great day. |

**That is the end of part one. You will now have half a minute to check your answers.**

*(30 second gap)*

**Now turn to part two.**

**Part two. You will hear a man giving some people information about a holiday park. First you have some time to look at questions eleven to fifteen.**

*(20 second gap)*

**Now listen carefully to the information talk and answer questions eleven to fifteen.**

Good morning, everyone. I'm Mr. Jenkins. I'd like to welcome you all today to our holiday park. Now you've all just spent the first night in your rooms and I hope you had a restful night. What I'd like to do is to tell you a little bit about the holiday park and what we have on offer for you.

As you may be aware, right now we're at the central coffee bar in the holiday park's main building, which is known as the Johnson Building. This is a large building in the very centre of the park. The coffee bar here is open every day **(Q11-Q15)** from six a.m. until eight p.m. It serves coffees, teas and other infusions, along with a variety of cold drinks and hot and cold snacks. It does not serve proper meals. For that, you'll need to go to one of our other restaurants, such as our pizzeria, French bistro or Asian street café elsewhere in the park. More of that later. Also available in this building is the main reception **(Q11-Q15)**. If you have any questions about the park, just go there and speak to our receptionists. One exception to this is anything to do with money. If you need to pay any bills or enquire about any costs, you'll need to go the finance office, which is in a separate building two hundred metres down the drive towards the main entrance. The maintenance team are also based there, so go there if there's anything wrong in your rooms or if you see anything faulty in the park. Back to where we are now. On the second floor, you'll find the first aid centre **(Q11-Q15)**, which has a lovely view of the lake and our cinema, which can be seen at the far end of the lake. There, we show old and new movies that hopefully appeal to all ages and tastes. The first aid centre has a nurse on duty twenty-four hours a day. The nurse can also get you to the doctor's surgery around half an hour away if there is anything she can't deal with. The rest of the second floor is taken up with various administration offices. On the floor above that is our Fitness Area **(Q11-Q15)**, which you can use at any time if you're over eighteen years of age. The Fitness Area does not include our saunas, steam rooms and treatment areas, which are found next to the main swimming pool. In the Fitness Area, you can work out on your own or book a session with one of our instructors. If you're feeling lazy, just go to our Internet café, which is next to the Fitness Area **(Q11-Q15)**. You can comfortably surf the net with a hot chocolate while watching the more motivated people work out!

**You now have some time to look at questions sixteen to twenty.**

*(20 second gap)*

**Now listen to the rest of the information talk and answer questions sixteen to twenty.**

We have plenty of activities for you and your family to enjoy. I'll describe some of these now.

In the south of the park is our water park complex. It's a ten-pound entrance fee for the public, but free for residents. Also, this area is open to the public in the afternoons, but in the mornings, it's reserved for the residents **(Q16)** of the holiday park and that's you. The water park opens from nine in the morning and closes at six in the late afternoon. The resident-only time changes at midday.

We also have a mini-golf, which is open from nine a.m. to six p.m. You don't need to own any equipment. Just turn up and we'll supply everything. The mini-golf can be quite busy, so we limit the number of people on the area at any one time. Groups of maximum five people are allowed to start playing at five-minute **(Q17)** intervals. Reservations are not permitted, so it's run on a first come, first play basis. There's no cost for the mini-golf.

For the keep-fit amongst you, we run a jogging club, which meets twice a day. The first session is at eight a.m. and covers a distance of around four **(Q18)** kilometres. The jog goes through the forest on easy flat trails. The second session is at five p.m. and is longer, at six kilometres. This also goes through the forest on well-tended trails, but is hillier and more demanding.  Both the jogs are led by two of our fitness instructors. One will lead the jog and the other will bring up the rear. The sessions start with some warming-up exercises **(Q19)** and end with stretching.

Not far away is the historic town of Levington. With its medieval castle and the historic old town with the old fortified walls still standing, this is a popular visiting place for our guests. We have a minibus service that goes to Levington every day at one p.m. and returns at five p.m. There's an extra cost of two pounds return for this service. Tickets can be bought at the main reception area. You can also buy tickets from the bus driver **(Q20)**, but if all the tickets are sold, you may find yourself disappointed, so book ahead if you really want to go.

Before I carry on, are there any questions so far?

**That is the end of part two. You will now have half a minute to check your answers.**

*(30 second gap)*

**Now turn to part three.**

**Part three. You will hear a student giving his presentation and interacting with his university teacher. First you have some time to look at questions twenty-one to twenty-five.**

*(20 second gap)*

**Now listen carefully and answer questions twenty-one to twenty-five.**

Alex    Good morning, Professor Norris. We're all here now.

Professor Norris       Thanks, Alex. Good morning everyone. Today, we're going to hear from Alex, who is going to do his presentation. First of all, I'd like to tell you that <u>next week's seminar on your next essay</u> **(Q21)** is not in this room, but in room four two five in the history department. It's the room that has all the pictures of the Great Wall of China in it. We're doing a swap with the history department for just that day, so that they can use this larger room, which will suit their purposes. Now, Alex. Are you ready?

Alex     Yes, thank you, Professor Norris. I'm ready.

Professor Norris       So, what do you plan to talk about today?

Alex     Well, many of you will have heard of the Forest of Dean.

Professor Norris       Let everyone know where it is, just in case.

Alex     It's on the borders of south Wales and England, near the River Severn, which is the longest river in the UK.

Professor Norris       Thank you. Now, what are you going to tell us about the Forest of Dean?

Alex     I'd like to focus today on the new colonies of wild boar that have sprung up in the forest. These are wild pigs, if you didn't know. <u>This fits in with our course subject, which explores how new non-indigenous species can affect a natural environment</u> **(Q22)**.

Professor Norris       Surely wild boars are native to the UK though?

Alex     They were, but they went extinct here around seven hundred years ago. I know it's not quite the same, but seven hundred years is a long time and the forest environment adapted to the boars' absence. It's pretty much the same as if a foreign species were introduced.

Professor Norris       Yes. I think I agree with that.

Alex     So, boars were once common in the Forest of Dean and were hunted for food. In medieval times, boars from the royal forest were supplied for the King's table. There is a record of an order for a hundred boars and sows for a Christmas feast in twelve fifty-four. <u>Boars are thought to have become extinct in Britain due to over-hunting not long after this time, although disease also was a more minor factor</u> **(Q23)**. The farming of wild boars in Britain became fashionable in the nineteen seventies, but <u>the principal issue facing the industry was that it was not particularly profitable</u> **(Q24)**. In nineteen ninety-nine, boars escaped, or were released, from a farm near the Forest of Dean. In two thousand and four, a group of about sixty farm-raised boars were dumped near the forest.

Professor Norris       Really! So many boar escaped from one farm!

Alex     No. In the second case, the boar were released. A farm was going out of business and it was easier for them to just release the boar rather than go through the selling process.

Professor Norris       Were they prosecuted?

Alex     I'm afraid I don't know. I just focused on the boars.

Professor Norris       That's OK. It's not important.

Alex    Anyway, very soon it was clear that the two released populations had merged and, in spite of worries by the Forestry Commission regarding limited bloodlines, a healthy breeding population was surviving in the forest. The breeding has caused the population to grow steadily and there is now believed to be in excess of eight hundred boars in the Forest of Dean **(Q25)**, with the population expanding out into neighbouring areas. Boar are now feral throughout the forest area and the Forest of Dean population is the largest of the breeding populations that now exist in England.

**You now have some time to look at questions twenty-six to thirty.**

*(20 second gap)*

**Now listen to the rest of the presentation and answer questions twenty-six to thirty.**

Alex    The problem with the released and breeding wild boars in the Forest of Dean is that the population is getting too large.

Professor Norris        Who is actually responsible for controlling the population?

Alex    That's an interesting legal point. Once the animals escaped, the government's position is that free roaming wild boars are feral wild animals and as such do not belong to anyone, and that responsibility for managing wild boars rests with the land owner **(Q26)**. Thus, feral wild boars have the status of a wild animal, such as wild deer, and foxes.

Professor Norris        What will happen to the excess numbers then?

Alex    Well, many people feel that the numbers are not a problem. Although there are stories of wild boars being dangerous, locals next to the Forest of Dean say this is not the case. When wild boars are disturbed by walkers, the tendency is for one of the larger sows to position themselves between the walkers and the young, often accompanied by much snorting, whilst the family group **(Q27)** leads the young to safety. Once the family has moved off, the defending sow will usually suddenly turn and run off to rejoin the group. The defending sow may well also be provoked into a mock charge at the intruding people, particularly if that group continue to approach for a better look, or simply because they have not noticed the boars. Male boars can be more aggressive, but so far there are only stories of dogs being chased.

Professor Norris        I don't expect that the government have accepted the stories of locals!

Alex    Absolutely not. There are now regular culls of the wild boar population by the Forestry Commission in the Forest of Dean. Forest rangers **(Q28)** on specific days go out and destroy carefully selected numbers of the animals. The problem is that animal rights activists object to the culls and try to disrupt them.

Professor Norris        Can't the forest just be closed on cull days?

Alex    No, the forest is open land. The activists know that the forest rangers conducting the cull have to stay close to big paths, so that they can bring vehicles to move the dead carcasses of the animals away. The activists just divide the forest up and watch over the big paths **(Q29)** and make lots of noise and move bait.

Professor Norris        Are the activists successful?

Alex    To a certain extent, yes. It's a big forest and they can't be everywhere, but they create enough disruption that they have spoiled quite a few of the planned cull days. The forests rangers are quite annoyed about this and point out that the large numbers of wild boar can affect the lives of other inhabitants of the forest. The forest rangers haven't given up though and they now keep the cull dates secret **(Q30)** and try and catch the activists unprepared.

**That is the end of part three. You will now have half a minute to check your answers.**

*(30 second gap)*

**Now turn to part four.**

**Part four. You will hear part of an environmental science lecture on bottom trawling fishing in New Zealand. First you have some time to look at questions thirty-one to forty.**

*(50 second gap)*

**Now listen carefully and answer questions thirty-one to forty.**

Good morning. Today in this environmental sciences lecture, we are going to look at bottom trawling, and we will focus this time on our own waters here in New Zealand.

The area of ocean and seabed out to two hundred nautical miles from New Zealand's coastline is called the exclusive economic zone, or EEZ. This area covers approximately three point nine million square kilometres and is the fifth largest EEZ in the world. The depth of the sea within this area can extend to ten thousand **(Q31)** metres. The marine landscapes within New Zealand's EEZ include spectacular underwater mountains, valleys, geysers, and muddy flats. These are home to corals, sponges, and other unique forms of marine life.

Fishing can damage the seabed and the corals, sponges and other life found there, particularly when bottom-trawl or dredge fishing gear is used. How much damage occurs depends on a number of factors, including the type of seabed habitat that is being fished and the particular equipment **(Q32)** being used.

Conservation groups say bottom-trawling is the most destructive type of fishing undertaken in the world's oceans today. Bottom trawling involves dragging huge, heavy nets along the sea floor. Large metal plates and rubber wheels attached to these nets move along the bottom and crush nearly everything in their path. The bottom trawling net indiscriminately catches every life and object it encounters. Thus, many creatures end up mistakenly caught and thrown overboard dead or dying, including endangered fish and even vulnerable deep-sea corals, which can live for several hundred years. This collateral damage, which is known as the by-catch **(Q33)**, can amount to ninety percent of a trawl's total catch. Conservationists claim that all evidence indicates that deep-water life forms are very slow to recover from such damage, taking decades to hundreds of years, if they recover at all. Commercial fishing companies **(Q34)**, not surprisingly, tell a different story.

All human activity has some degree of impact on the natural environment. What is important is that these activities are closely monitored to ensure that impacts are managed and kept to an acceptable level. The New Zealand Ministry of Fisheries says it closely monitors bottom trawling as part of a comprehensive fisheries management regime. In New Zealand, one of the ways this is achieved on land is by setting aside large areas as national parks, where activities such as intensive farming are not permitted. In the marine environment, the approach is no different **(Q35)**. In 2007, the New Zealand Government, with the support of the fishing industry, closed one point one million square kilometres of seabed to bottom trawling and dredging, which is close to a third of New Zealand's entire EEZ. The seventeen separate closed areas, known as benthic protection areas, or BPA's, mainly cover areas of New Zealand waters that have never been trawled **(Q36)**. The seabed within these areas is largely in an untouched state and includes the full range of deep-sea underwater landscapes that occur across the EEZ. In addition to the BPA's, eighteen areas around underwater seamounts and geysers have been closed to all types of trawling, because of the unique marine life that is found there. Across New Zealand's EEZ, half of all known seamounts and all known active hydrothermal vents are closed to all trawling **(Q37)**.

In addition to the BPA's, the New Zealand Ministry of Fisheries says most of the New Zealand EEZ is deeper than one thousand two hundred and fifty metres and there is very little bottom trawling below that depth in New Zealand. Scientists have recently calculated that in excess of ninety-one per cent **(Q38)** of the New Zealand EEZ has never been bottom trawled. Finally, the New Zealand Ministry of Fisheries says it also regularly monitors where fishing vessels have operated, and the type and quantity of marine species, such as corals and sponges, which are caught.

New Zealand claims it is a world leader in successfully managing the effects that bottom trawling has on the seabed, closing one of the largest areas of marine space to bottom trawling in the world. Conservation groups are not happy with the New Zealand government though. They say that the ban doesn't extend to all vulnerable ecosystems **(Q39)**, and that some of the areas covered have already been fished out or are too deep to bottom trawl anyway. Of course, one third protection that the New Zealand government is so proud of leaves the two thirds unprotected and even if one third of a particular environment is protected, the damage inflicted in the other two thirds does have an impact on the rest. Conservation groups say that the only real way to protect the seabeds is to ban bottom trawling altogether and that if this means that consumers have to pay more for their fish, then this is a reasonable price to pay to preserve the underwater environment surrounding New Zealand. A final less noticed effect, but extremely important none the less, is that small community economies **(Q40)** are affected, as their fishermen's catch sizes are strongly affected by the enormous takes of industrial trawlers.

**That is the end of part four. You will now have half a minute to check your answers.**

*(30 second gap)*

**That is the end of listening test three.**

## LISTENING TEST 4 TRANSCRIPT

**This recording is copyright by Robert Nicholson and Simone Braverman, all rights reserved.**

**IELTS listening practice tests. Test four. In the IELTS test you hear some recordings and you have to answer questions on them. You have time to read the instructions and questions and check your work. All recordings are played only once. The test is in four parts. Now turn to part one.**

**Part one. You will hear a conversation between a man and a woman as the woman changes her family's hotel reservation.**

**First you have some time to look at questions one to five.**

*(20 second gap)*

**Now we begin. You should answer the questions as you listen, as the recording is not played twice. Listen carefully to the conversation and answer questions one to five.**

| | |
|---|---|
| Jake | The Sutherland Hotel. Jake speaking. How can I help you? |
| Mrs. Easton | Hello, my name is Mrs. Jane Easton. I have a reservation with you for next week, but I'd like to make a change. |
| Jake | OK. Do you have the reservation number with you? |
| Mrs. Easton | Yes. It's EZT four eight six, nine seven eight. |
| Jake | OK. I have your details here. I just need to take some details from you in order to confirm your identity. First of all, can you tell me your full name again? |
| Mrs. Easton | It's Mrs. Jane Easton. Easton is spelled <u>E - A - S - T - O - N</u> **(Q1)**. |
| Jake | And can I have your full address, including the postcode? |
| Mrs. Easton | It's <u>thirty</u> **(Q2)** Richmond Rise, Birkdale, Auckland. The postcode is oh six two six. |
| Jake | And can I have your date of birth, please? |
| Mrs. Easton | It's the fourteenth <u>October</u> **(Q3)** nineteen eighty-five. |
| Jake | Now, there's a couple of things missing from the reservation details. Can I ask you about them quickly, please? |
| Mrs. Easton | Yes, of course. |
| Jake | How did you find out about us? |
| Mrs. Easton | I found you in an Internet search. |

Jake              What website did you use?

Mrs. Easton              It was hotels.com **(Q4)**. I always use this website when I'm looking for hotels.

Jake              Yes. We get a lot of bookings from that website.

Mrs. Easton              They're very good. I have never had a bad experience using them.

Jake              And do you know if the website charged you a commission **(Q5)** for getting you the booking with us?

Mrs. Easton              No. It was clear from the start that they only received that from you. I paid nothing to them.

Jake              Thanks very much.

**Before the conversation continues, you have some time to look at questions six to ten.**

*(20 second gap)*

**Now listen carefully and answer questions six to ten.**

Jake              That's lovely, Mrs. Easton. Now, what can I do for you? You said you needed to change your reservation. Let me know what needs to be done and I'll make the changes and confirm everything by email.

Mrs. Easton              Thank you. At present, I have a reservation for myself and my husband, Michael. We've decided that we're going to bring our children with us now.

Jake              That's no problem. Can you give me the details of them with their ages?

Mrs. Easton              There are two of them, both boys. Mark is thirteen **(Q6)** and Max is eight.

Jake              Would you like separate rooms for the boys?

Mrs. Easton              No, just one twin room is fine for them both.

Jake              Now, you and your husband have a sea view. Do you want that for your children's room? A sea view is more expensive, of course.

Mrs. Easton              No. We don't need a sea view **(Q7)** for them. They'll just be sleeping there.

Jake              Is there anything else?

Mrs. Easton              Yes, I need to change the dates. At present, we're coming on Friday the twenty-second of May. As we're bringing the children, we won't be able to get to you until the following day. We planned to stay until the following Wednesday and we won't change that.

Jake              So, I just need to add the extra room for the boys and take off one day from the start of the booking.

Mrs. Easton    That's right. Can you let me know the new price?

Jake    Let me look. You and your husbands' price is one day cheaper. For the boys, Mark gets charged the full rate, but Max gets the child rate. Your old price was one thousand two hundred dollars and the new one is two thousand dollars **(Q8)** exactly. That includes all the local and district taxes.

Mrs. Easton    Can I get a receipt for that?

Jake    I can't do that for you now, but of course you'll be issued one when at the hotel.

Mrs. Easton    I think that's everything, then.

Jake    OK, Mrs Peters. Let me just check everything. So, the booking is held with your VISA card with the last four numbers eight five three seven. Is that still alright?

Mrs. Easton    Yes. That's fine. Do I need to add to the deposit **(Q9)** I've paid?

Jake    No, what you've paid already is fine.

Mrs. Easton    Will the hotel know that I've paid it?

Jake    Oh yes. Don't worry about that. It's all in the system. Now, as I said earlier, I'll send you a confirmation by email. I have your address already in the system. Now, is there anything else?

Mrs. Easton    Actually, yes. I've just thought of something. Is breakfast **(Q10)** included for everyone?

Jake    Yes. You all get that included in the price. Anything else?

Mrs. Easton    No. I think that's everything. Thanks very much for your help.

Jake    You're welcome. Goodbye.

Mrs. Easton    Goodbye.

**That is the end of part one. You will now have half a minute to check your answers.**

*(30 second gap)*

**Now turn to part two.**

**Part two. You will hear a man giving some people information about a tour of a chocolate factory. First you have some time to look at questions eleven to fifteen.**

*(20 second gap)*

**Now listen carefully to the information talk and answer questions eleven to fifteen.**

Good morning, everyone. My name's Marcus and I've been asked to tell you a little about tours around our chocolate factory.

The chocolate factory has always been a family business and it was constructed in 1924 **(Q11)**. We found there was a demand for guided tours a few years ago, as our brand is so well known that people want to have a look at how we operate here.

The factory does not operate twenty-four hours a day. It has done in the past, but it's not needed right now. The factory employs twenty-five **(Q12)** people full time. This includes the operating and maintenance staff, who are responsible for making the chocolate, and the office staff, who are responsible for marketing, finance and all other aspects of our business.

I'll now tell you what you see when you come on a tour. We meet in the reception area of the administration area. Here you will be given some orientation, a visitor's badge and a sterile hair net that must be worn in the manufacturing area, so that we keep in line with our hygiene policy. There will also be a short safety talk by our health and safety **(Q13)** officer.

The tour starts with seeing where the raw chocolate arrives. We don't refine the raw material from the cacao bean. The raw chocolate is melted down in enormous vats. Depending on which product is being manufactured, different ingredients **(Q14)** are blended. These include milk, sugar, lecithin, which is an emulsifier, vanilla, cinnamon, fruits and nuts and chili, as well as others. Every time we change the product, the vats must be thoroughly cleaned, especially if we've been using chili.

The manufacturing machinery creates the different shapes of the product and you'll see whatever product is being manufactured at the time of your visit. Finally, the last part of the manufacturing process is the wrapping **(Q15)**. We use a foil and paper combination in two pieces, which is done on a horizontal flow wrapping machine. Foil is necessary to stop greasy cocoa butter getting from the inside of the package to the outside and the paper of course is branded on the outside to look attractive.

**You now have some time to look at questions sixteen to twenty.**

*(20 second gap)*

**Now listen to the rest of the information talk and answer questions sixteen to twenty.**

After the manufacturing process, you will return to the administration area. You will get to watch a film on the history of chocolate and then there will be a short lecture **(Q16)** that goes through the marketing and sales strategies of our firm. Of course, we don't give away any of our secrets!

At the end of the visit, you will of course get a tasting! All of our products will be available to taste and your guide **(Q17)** will assist you in choosing a selection. We recommend, especially with children, that you don't eat too much. As well as being too unhealthy, your bodies are not usually ready for so much rich food and it can upset your stomachs.

So, let me run through some administration for you. First of all, for individuals and small groups, we have one tour in the morning, starting at <u>ten</u> **(Q18)** a.m. and one in the afternoon, starting at two p.m. For these tours, adults pay <u>thirteen</u> **(Q19)** dollars, senior citizens pay nine dollars and children pay six dollars. Of course, we run larger groups and school tours as well. The usual fees apply, except for school tours. Children cost four dollars each and for every seven children there must be one member of the school staff. There's no charge for the staff. All our guides, by the way, have police screening for working with children. Larger tours can take place at any time during the day, though of course they must be booked in advance. We have free parking for cars and coaches and the whole factory is <u>wheelchair</u> **(Q20)** friendly. Guide dogs are welcome, except in the manufacturing areas for obvious reasons.

**That is the end of part two. You will now have half a minute to check your answers.**

*(30 second gap)*

**Now turn to part three.**

**Part three. You will hear two students discussing a course change with their tutor. First you have some time to look at questions twenty-one to twenty-five.**

*(20 second gap)*

**Now listen carefully and answer questions twenty-one to twenty-five.**

Edward          Professor Holden. Do you have a minute?

Professor Holden       Yes. Come in, both of you. What can I do for you?

Tina          We wanted to ask you about changing courses.

Professor Holden       Ah. Well, sit down for a while then. So, you two are studying history at the moment, is that right?

Edward          That's right.

Professor Holden       And why do you want to change?

Tina          Well, you know how in the first year, we had to study three different subjects, one of which was our main one?

Professor Holden       Yes. That's our way of making sure that you get a broader education. You can also have the chance to see if a different subject might suit you better.

Tina          That's what has happened to me. In my first year, I studied history, French and linguistics. Now it's the start of the second year, and I've found that it is the linguistics that I really miss. History is great, but I've found that there were too many <u>periods</u> **(Q21)** to study that I'm just not interested in.

Professor Holden       Have you talked to any of the History department about this? Have you found out all the syllabus for the next two years?

Tina          Yes. I've spoken to the head of department and got the whole schedule. I also spoke to the course secretary and some of the lecturers.

Page 181

Professor Holden     Do you know that in years two and three, you don't need to study everything? You can choose the periods that you find more interesting.

Tina          Yes, I know. The course secretary went through everything with me very carefully. The problem is that year three has most of the specialisation **(Q22)** and even then I'll have too many obligatory topics.

Professor Holden     What about you, Edward?

Edward       Well, I studied History, English and Earth Sciences. I chose Earth sciences, as I wanted one subject that would be really different to what I was used to. I was really good at sciences at school, so I didn't find it difficult at all.

Professor Holden     So, is that what you want to study now, or is it English?

Edward       I love the English and the History, but I can't handle all the essays **(Q23)** in both subjects.

Professor Holden     Yes, I understand that. But, are you sure that you will handle the change of choice from a main subject in the arts to one that is so different in the sciences?

Edward       I've thought about this all summer. I know it's a big switch, but I've done some extra reading **(Q24)** over the summer and I talked it over with my family.

Professor Holden     Have you spoken to any of the Earth Sciences department about it?

Edward       Oh yes. I spoke to a lot of the teachers and they asked me about my education background. They seemed to be satisfied that I could cope.

Professor Holden     I'm not so sure.

Edward       Well, I can't ever be totally sure, but it's what I really want to do. I know it'll be hard work. Earth sciences has more lectures, but the major assessments are smaller assignments and projects **(Q25)**. The exams are shorter, too.

**You now have some time to look at questions twenty-six to thirty.**

*(20 second gap)*

**Now listen to the rest of the discussion and answer questions twenty-six to thirty.**

Professor Holden     In order to change, there is a certain amount of paperwork. Both of you need first of all to fill in this form. You need to put the main subject you're studying and the subject that you want to study. You'll need some signatures on it, too.

Tina          Whose do we need, Professor Holden?

Professor Holden     You'll need your personal tutor's signature. For you, Tina, that's me of course, but I don't know for Edward. I'm not his tutor.

Edward    It's Doctor Flynn **(Q26-Q28)**.

Professor Holden    OK. Now, you'll need as well the signatures of the head of department of the subject to which you're transferring. For you, Edward, you want to switch to Earth Sciences, don't you?

Edward    That's right. Mr. Thomas is the head of Earth Sciences.

Professor Holden    That's true, but he's not the head of University Science, who is the person you'll need. That's Professor Atkins **(Q26-Q28)**. She's very busy, but if you give the form to Mr. Morton, her PA, he'll make sure the form gets signed and back to you quickly. For Tina, your new HOD will be Professor Coles.

Tina    OK.

Professor Holden    Finally, you'll both need the signature of the director. You'll need to get Miss Morgan's signature for that **(Q26-Q28)**. Doctor Tennant is on long-term sick leave and Miss Morgan is his short-term fill-in.

Edward    And do we need the signature from the department that we're leaving?

Professor Holden    The HOD for history is Professor Evans, but he'll hear about it through normal channels. He doesn't need to take part in this process.

Edward    OK. Thanks.

Professor Holden    Now, do you know what to do with these forms once you have all the signatures?

Tina    No. Can't we just give it to you?

Professor Holden    You can come and ask me any questions, but don't leave the finished form with me. You need to take the form to the registrar's office.

Edward    Can we email it?

Professor Holden    I know scanning and emailing is a lot easier, but the registrar's office will need the original.

Tina    What about post then?

Professor Holden    Posting is fine **(Q29)**. However, that might delay things. These kinds of changes can only be done quite near the start of the second year. If your paper gets lost in the post or stuck over a weekend, it might not work for you.

Tina    OK. How do we go there then?

Professor Holden    Go down to the railway station. Go past it and on the right will be the university administrative building. It faces the post office. Go to the second floor and ask if the registrar's office is open. It is often closed. If they tell you it's open, go up a floor to where it is and deliver your form **(Q30)**.

**That is the end of part three. You will now have half a minute to check your answers.**

*(30 second gap)*

Page 183

**Now turn to part four.**

**Part four. You will hear part of a geography lecture on Australia's Great Artesian Basin. First you have some time to look at questions thirty-one to forty.**

*(50 second gap)*

**Now listen carefully and answer questions thirty-one to forty.**

Good morning ladies and gentleman and welcome to this geography lecture.

Occupying an area of over one point seven million square kilometres beneath the arid and semi-arid parts of Queensland, New South Wales, South Australia and the Northern Territory, the Great Artesian Basin covers almost a quarter of the Australian continent, and contains enough water to cover the world over. Much remains to be known about this valuable resource that has enabled life in inland Australia to develop over thousands of years.

To explain how the Great Artesian Basin works, you need to know how it came to exist in the first place. Back in the Triassic age, Australia was joined together with the other southern continents, including Antarctica, South America, Africa and New Zealand, in a land mass called Gondwana. Right up in the north west corner of Gondwana, there was a <u>natural dip</u> **(Q31)** that became the Great Artesian Basin. Over the next one hundred million years, huge events like ice ages in Europe and tectonic plate movements caused the ocean level to rise and fall. When the ocean levels rose, water became trapped in that natural dip and formed a sea. But when the ocean levels fell, the whole area became land again. When the seas drained away, they left <u>clay</u> **(Q32)** deposits behind, which hardened into impermeable stone strata.

These stone strata residues became the environment that allowed the formation of the Great Artesian Basin. Below ground level, where the ancient natural dip lies today, there is a layer of permeable stone allowing falling rain to seep through it. Where there is no impermeable stone, the water soaks down until it reaches <u>the saturation level</u> **(Q33)**, which is where the rock ends and the water reservoir of the Basin begins. The water in the reservoir is then held between two impermeable stone strata. This water is incredibly pure, as it has been filtered and cleaned as it passed from the permeable rock. The water then remains trapped under the ground, only emerging through <u>a natural spring</u> **(Q34)**.

Scientists estimate that there's over sixty-five thousand million megalitres of water in the Basin right now. A megalitre is a million litres. Sixty thousand million megalitres would be enough to cover all the land on the planet in almost half a metre of water. The water fortunately does not stay underground. For thousands and thousands of years, artesian water has been bubbling up to the surface all over the Basin area. This brings life to parts of Australia that would otherwise be barren desert. These areas are home to a host of native plant and animal species that have evolved in these unusual <u>ecosystems</u> **(Q35)**. Many of these can't be found anywhere else in the world. What's more, water from the Basin's springs around the recharge zones often seeps into natural creek and river systems, helping to keep them flowing when the rains don't come. Of course, not all the emerging water comes from natural escape. Farmers, town councils and others all create bore holes to make artesian wells and these have helped maintain agriculture and <u>urbanisation</u> **(Q36)** that wouldn't have been otherwise possible.

The trouble is that modern usage of the Basin's water has caused the Great Artesian Basin problems. It's so bad that a lot of bores and natural springs have simply stopped flowing, and hundreds of bores that do flow are out of control. They can't be turned off, and they're wasting millions of litres of water every day. A lot of bore water flows into shallow channels dug into the dirt, which encourage noxious weeds and feral animals, and it's almost pointless, because the open channels or drains mean around ninety-five per cent of the water evaporates **(Q37)** or seeps away before it can even be used. Meanwhile, to make matters worse, a lot of old bores were poorly made, or the casings underground are corroding, so the water is escaping to the wrong places and damaging the environment.

There are, however, things we can do. These days, there's a strategy in place to fix up the old bores so they can be used in a sustainable way, and the water can be distributed more responsibly. This process involves what we call capping and piping. Put simply, capping is just like putting a lid on the bores. Through a tap system **(Q38)**, farmers can turn the bores on and off and only use the water when it's needed. Piping involves replacing the old open channels or drains with new piping. Although this is a lengthy and expensive process, it is regarded as one of the best ways to preserve a lot of the water that is needlessly lost. Government funding has allowed the process of piping to be carried out for a number of years now and, because of this, the water goes straight to tanks **(Q39)** without being wasted, and it doesn't ruin the native landscape by encouraging weeds and feral animals.

This effort to make the water usage is vital. The Great Artesian Basin is key to life to about a quarter of the country, but it also impacts Australians from coast to coast. In fact, it impacts the country so much that if it was to dry up, Australia would be a very different place. Seventy towns that still rely on the Basin for their water would disappear. The beef, wool and sheep industries would lose about one billion Australian dollars a year, and the food production system would be affected very badly. Australia would have to import more food and the balance of payments **(Q40)** would change affecting the country's economy as a whole.

**That is the end of part four. You will now have half a minute to check your answers.**

*(30 second gap)*

**That is the end of listening test four.**

## LISTENING TEST 5 TRANSCRIPT

**This recording is copyright by Robert Nicholson and Simone Braverman, all rights reserved.**

**IELTS listening practice tests. Test five. In the IELTS test you hear some recordings and you have to answer questions on them. You have time to read the instructions and questions and check your work. All recordings are played only once. The test is in four parts. Now turn to part one.**

**Part one. You will hear a conversation between a man and a woman discussing a train ticket.**

**First you have some time to look at questions one to five.**

*(20 second gap)*

**Now we begin. You should answer the questions as you listen, as the recording is not played twice. Listen carefully to the conversation and answer questions one to five.**

| | |
|---|---|
| Roger | Good morning. Welcome to Southern Trains. What can I do for you today? |
| Sandra | Good morning. Can I get train tickets here? |
| Roger | Yes, you can. |
| Sandra | Good. I'd like to buy a season ticket, please. |
| Roger | That's no problem. First of all, I'd like to take some personal information. |
| Sandra | OK. |
| Roger | So, what is your full name? |
| Sandra | I'm Sandra Williams. That's S - A - N - D - R - A and then <u>W - I - L - L - I - A - M - S</u> **(Q1)**. |
| Roger | Thank you. And can I have your full address, including the postal code? |
| Sandra ED. | It's <u>forty-three</u> **(Q2)** Andover Way. The town is Stanton and the postal code is ST six, three |
| Roger | Thank you. Now I need your date of birth. |
| Sandra | It's the eighth of October, <u>nineteen ninety-four</u> **(Q3)**. |
| Roger | Have you had a season ticket with us before? |
| Sandra | No, this is the first time. |
| Roger | That's fine. Now, your season ticket can be registered online. To set up an account, we send you an email with details of what to do. So, can I have your email address, please? |
| Sandra | I'm not that keen on giving out my email address. I get too much spam. |

Roger    I can understand that. I can assure you that we don't send you any other emails at all and the address is kept confidential. We are bound to that by law.

Sandra    I suppose that's OK. My address is sandra at primrose dot com. Primrose is spelled <u>P - R - I - M - R - O - S - E</u> **(Q4)**.

Roger    And finally, I need a contact number for you.

Sandra    Is it OK if I just give you my cell number?

Roger    Yes, that's fine.

Sandra    It's oh five <u>four eight two</u> **(Q5)**, four nine five, seven one two.

Roger    Thank you. That is all the personal information done then.

**Before the conversation continues, you have some time to look at questions six to ten.**

*(20 second gap)*

**Now listen carefully and answer questions six to ten.**

Roger    Now I need some details about the season ticket. What journey do you need it for?

Sandra    <u>I've just got a new job in Bexington and I've quit my old job in Petersfield. I was thinking of driving to the new job, but there's always too much traffic when you pass Amberton. I thought the train would therefore be better for the commute trip from here in Stanton</u> **(Q6)**.

Roger    I think you're right to do that. Trains don't get held up by traffic jams! Do you want just that route? For a little more, I can get you a ticket for the whole region.

Sandra    I'm not sure yet. I'll see when you give me the actual prices.

Roger    Of course. Now the price also depends on the timings. Off-peak is much cheaper of course. That's for leaving after nine thirty in the morning and for not returning between the hours of four and six in the afternoon.

Sandra    Saving money would be good, but <u>I'll need a peak ticket. I'll need to keep normal work hours and also not be too late back home to look after the children when they get back from school.</u>

Roger    <u>Another way to save would be to buy only a weekday season ticket and not travel on weekends. Would that be good for you?</u>

Sandra    <u>Let's think. I do have some family near my new job, but I don't think I'd travel too often by train at weekends there. I'd probably drive with the family. The weekday thing would be an excellent option for me</u> **(Q7)**.

Roger    OK. I'll make it that. Finally, would you like first class, second class or variable class?

Page 187

Sandra          What's the variable class?

Roger           That is something for frequent travellers. Travellers get twelve individual journeys a calendar month in first class and the rest of the month in second class. That way, you can treat yourself from time to time when you're tired or get some peace and quiet when the train is busy.

Sandra          I think I'll go for that **(Q8)**. I hate it when there are too many noisy kids on a train.

Roger           So, now for the prices. For a one-month ticket for your route it is one hundred and ninety-eight dollars. If you go for the whole region, it will be two hundred and fifteen dollars. If you want a ticket for more than one month, it's the same price per month, until you go for a ticket for six months or longer. Then there is a twenty per cent discount, which would make it one hundred and fifty-eight dollars and forty cents per month for your route, or one hundred and seventy-two dollars for the whole region.

Sandra          I think I'll just go for my route rather than the whole region, but I'll take a six month ticket and get the discount **(Q9)**.

Roger           That's fine. It'll be one hundred and fifty-eight forty then. I've just put in all the information. Please wait for a couple of minutes for the computer to process the order. The ticket will then be printed out.

Sandra          Where would I go to catch my train here every morning? Is it still platform four?

Roger           It used to be that one, but it's changed now to seven **(Q10)**. When you come in through the entrance, there are six platforms right in front of you. That's where platform four is. To get to yours, go right as you come in and you'll find it just beyond the wall on the right side of the station.

Sandra          OK.

**That is the end of part one. You will now have half a minute to check your answers.**

*(30 second gap)*

**Now turn to part two.**

**Part two. You will hear a woman giving some people information about some hotel services. First you have some time to look at questions eleven to fifteen.**

*(20 second gap)*

**Now listen carefully to the information talk and answer questions eleven to fifteen.**

Hello, everyone. My name is Anna. I'd like to welcome you all today to the Paradise Hotel and I'll tell you now a little about the services we have on offer here.

As you've probably noticed, the Paradise Hotel is built on a hill and so its design reflects that. Our hotel is on seven levels and I'd quickly like to explain what can be found on each level. The main entrance to the hotel and the reception is on level three. You can find the concierge's desk there **(Q11)** and also our coffee bar with its great view over the hotel's swimming pools, beach and sea. All our accommodation is on levels four, five and six. If your room is on level four, then its number will start with a four, for example four oh seven **(Q12)**, and if your room is on level five, then its number will start with a five, for example five two three. The same goes for level six. Level seven gives access to the spa and treatment area. If you'd like to book a treatment there or just use some of facilities, call it from the phone in your room or just go down and speak to the staff there. Level seven also gives access to the swimming pools and, beyond them, the beach **(Q13)**. Both the beach and the swimming pools have sun loungers, where you can lie and enjoy the good weather. There are also snack kiosks and bars found around the pools and beach.

Moving up from the reception level, level two is where all the hotel restaurants are. There are three to choose from. First, there is the Chef's restaurant, where you can eat breakfast, lunch and dinner from the buffets provided. If you'd prefer to eat á la carte, the Eastern restaurant does Asian specialities, such as Thai, Indian and Chinese food, and the Ocean restaurant specialises in seafood and fish **(Q14)**. Again, places can be booked for the Eastern and Ocean restaurants from your room phone or you can book at reception on level three or just go to the restaurant itself.

Level one has our Fitness Area. This includes a fully equipped gym with weights and aerobic machinery and class rooms, where you can go for scheduled fitness classes, such as aerobics, pilates, yoga or spinning **(Q15)**. The schedules are all posted at the Fitness Area's reception and at the main hotel reception.

**You now have some time to look at questions sixteen to twenty.**

*(20 second gap)*

**Now listen to the rest of the information talk and answer questions sixteen to twenty.**

Now I'd like to let you know about some of the things that are going on this week at the hotel.

Today's Monday and tonight we have an entertainment evening by the pool. The weather forecast is good and you should enjoy our selection of dancers, singers, magician and other acts. This will start at seven and go on until ten **(Q16)**.

Tomorrow, we have a pub style quiz, which will be held in the rooftop bar **(Q17)**. You can access this if you go up to the gym and follow the stairs opposite where the lift opens. The quiz will start at eight in the evening and go on for around two hours. Please note that under eighteens will not be allowed in the bar.

On Wednesday, we have a karaoke night. This will start at seven and go on until nine. This will take place next to the pool and you are invited to be brave, grab the microphone and show everyone what you can do. To start the evening, the hotel manager has bravely volunteered to sing first with his favourite song **(Q18)**. He hasn't told us what his song is yet!

We have left Thursday evening free. Some people just like to be left alone to relax and there is a travelling circus visiting the town and this is only one kilometre away. Let us know if you'd like us to book you a taxi to and back from the circus if you'd like to go.

Friday evening is our jazz night. We have a local jazz band who plays with us every week and they are a firm favourite with all our guests. This takes place in the coffee bar lounge and in order to see them, you need to book a table. We only have forty tables available with five places at each, so make sure you book ahead, so that you won't be disappointed. Booking a table costs thirty dollars and <u>bookings should be done at the reception</u> **(Q19)**, not the coffee bar.

Saturday and Sunday are also left free, though there will be <u>some live music playing both evenings by the pool</u> **(Q20)**, from seven until half past nine.

Now, I have posted this schedule of events on the entertainments noticeboard and it's also available on our hotel website. If you'd like to ask me any questions about anything, please do so at any time. I'm usually in my office, which is next to reception. If I'm not there, ask reception, and they'll page me.

**That is the end of part two. You will now have half a minute to check your answers.**

*(30 second gap)*

**Now turn to part three.**

**Part three. You will hear four students discussing their geography project. First you have some time to look at questions twenty-one to twenty-five.**

*(20 second gap)*

**Now listen carefully and answer questions twenty-one to twenty-five.**

| | |
|---|---|
| Tony | Hi Alison. How are you? |
| Alison | Hi Tony. I'm good. Are the other two here yet? |
| Tony | Not yet. Oh, here they are now. Hi Greg. Hi Sophie. |
| Greg | Hi Tony. Hi Alison. |
| Sophie | Hi guys! Are we late? |

Tony        Not at all. Well, let's get down to it right away. As you know, we're talking about our geography project today and our task is to survey an area to see whether it would be suitable for a new supermarket. Alison, you told me yesterday that you had an idea of how to start.

Alison        Yes. Well, the first thing is that we'll have to choose the actual site that we wish to survey. Once that's done, we'll need to do certain preparation work.

Greg        So, does anyone have any idea of a suitable site to survey? Sophie. You're good at this.

Sophie        Thanks, Greg. I've got some ideas. There is a farmer's field on Castle Road, just after the road leaves town and goes over the bridge. That could be a good place. Another possible site I found was in the town centre at the old cigarette factory. Finally, there's a possible site at the airport. Here are some notes I made for everyone. How's that, Greg?

Greg       Excellent. I like the one at the cigarette factory. That'll be great for people to go to without having to travel too far. I also think that <u>the town council</u> **(Q21)** would provide grants to help develop that site, as it's been abandoned for a long time.

Alison       That's true, Greg, but if you look at Sophie's notes, it says that the size of the site is limited. Not that many people will go on foot and, while there'll be enough room for the actual supermarket building, there'll be no room for a <u>car park</u> **(Q22)**.

Tony       That's a good point, Alison. The potential cost of the site will be a lot higher too, as it's in the town centre.

Greg       It's just a project, though. We won't actually need to buy a site.

Tony       No, but doing costs in the project will all be part of how we're assessed. We will need to look at all start-up costs, as well as <u>income forecasts</u> **(Q23)** for the first ten years of operation.

Greg       OK. I see that it's important.

Alison       I like the idea of the site by the river. It shouldn't be too expensive and the site near the edge of the town would be good for people to get to. There's the town's ring road that goes nearby the site as well.

Tony       Yes. However, the problem I see with that site is that it's too close to the river. We've had years with lots of rain recently and the river's been known to burst its banks. There would maybe have to be a great deal of <u>protection building</u> **(Q24)** to be done.

Alison       I suppose that would be something that our survey would address.

Sophie       In fact, that might be something extra for us to explore that we wouldn't normally have the opportunity to study. It could work in our favour.

Greg       And now the airport site?

Tony       It seems there's nothing particularly challenging about that site. The land wouldn't be too expensive and there's plenty of <u>road access</u> **(Q25)** because of the people going to the airport.

Sophie       Actually, I heard airport sites can be quite expensive.

Greg       Yes. And although there is plenty of road access, the airport is not actually that close to the town. It's not that convenient.

**You now have some time to look at questions twenty-six to thirty.**

*(20 second gap)*

**Now listen to the rest of the discussion and answer questions twenty-six to thirty.**

Tony       So, I think we all agree on the Castle Road site next to the river. So, Sophie. What's next?

Sophie    We really need to decide who does what. There are a number of jobs to be done before we actually get to go to the field and survey it. If we can get everything done quickly, we can do the survey at the weekend.

Greg    So, what's the first thing?

Sophie    We need to get authorisation from the farmer to be on his land. If we can't do that, there's no point in starting to gather any information **(Q26)**.

Alison    I can do that. I'll nip down to the town surveyor's office and find the name and address of the owner. I'll go straight away and talk to him or her.

Sophie    Thanks, Alison. Now, one of the important early things is to find out whether there are any other development plans scheduled for that specific area or in any other area that would affect what we're planning.

Greg    I can try and do that, but I'm not sure what the procedure is **(Q27)**.

Tony    It's easy, Greg. You just go down to the surveyor's office again and ask for all proposed plans for that postcode. I can text you the postcode later.

Greg    Thanks, Tony **(Q28)**. That's my job organised then.

Sophie    Now, when we start to survey the field, we'll need certain equipment. You asked about equipment, didn't you, Alison?

Alison    I spoke to Professor Johnson yesterday and we can borrow all the necessary equipment from the department. I'll check that all the equipment is free at the weekend **(Q29)**.

Greg    Good. Anything else?

Alison    Yes, Professor Johnson also told me that we have to pay a two hundred pound deposit for the equipment.

Greg    I don't have that kind of money.

Tony    I can pay the deposit as long as I get it back. My parents have just put some money in the bank from a job I did for the summer **(Q30)**. I can get it from the bank when we need it.

Alison    It should only be for two days, Tony. We can get everything done in that time.

Tony    OK. I'll pay the deposit and pick up the equipment from the department.

Alison    Don't get it just yet. We have to get the authorisation to be on the land first.

Tony    OK.

Sophie    So, if we can get all these jobs done over the next three days, we can meet again on Thursday. If all is OK, we could get the equipment on Friday and survey the field at the weekend.

| | |
|---|---|
| Alison | Good. |
| Greg | Well, thanks everyone. I'd better be off. Bye. |
| Sophie | Bye. |
| Alison | Bye. |

**That is the end of part three. You will now have half a minute to check your answers.**

*(30 second gap)*

**Now turn to part four.**

**Part four. You will hear part of a lecture on tea. First you have some time to look at questions thirty-one to forty.**

*(50 second gap)*

**Now listen carefully and answer questions thirty-one to forty.**

Today's lecture is about a product that has become a social custom in many countries: tea.

Tea is first recorded as being drunk in China **(Q31)**, with the first records of it dating from around two hundred years BC. In fact, tea drinking certainly became established in China many centuries before it had even been heard of in the west. In the latter half of the sixteenth century, there are the first mentions of tea as a drink among Europeans. These are mostly from Portuguese, who were living in the East as traders and missionaries. Although some of these individuals may have brought back samples of tea to their native country, it was not the Portuguese who were the first to ship back tea as a commercial import. This was done by the Dutch, who in the last years of the sixteenth century began to encroach on Portuguese trading routes **(Q32)** in the East.

In the seventeenth century, the British took to tea with an enthusiasm that continues to the present day. It became a popular drink in coffee houses, which were as much locations for the transaction of business, as they were for relaxation or pleasure. Coffee houses were thought to be the preserve of middle- and upper-class men, as women drank tea in their own homes, and then tea was still too expensive to be widespread among the working classes. In part, its high price was due to a punitive system of tax. The first tax **(Q33)** on tea in the leaf, introduced in Britain in 1689, was so high at twenty-five pence per pound that it almost stopped sales. It was gradually reduced until as recently as 1964, when tea tax was finally abolished. British politicians were forever tinkering with the exact rate and method.

During the eighteenth century, there was an equally furious argument about whether tea drinking was good or bad for the health. Wealthy philanthropists in particular worried that excessive tea drinking among the working classes would lead to weakness and melancholy. Typically, they were not concerned with the continuing popularity of tea among the wealthy classes, for whom strength for labour was of rather less importance! The debate rumbled on into the nineteenth century, but was really put to an end in the middle of that century, when a new generation of wealthy philanthropists realised the value of tea drinking to the temperance movement. In their enthusiasm to have the working classes go teetotal, tea was regularly offered at temperance meetings as a substitute for <u>alcohol</u> **(Q34)**.

Today, tea is a staggeringly popular drink all over the world. Although many people perceive the UK to be the biggest tea consumer, they only make up <u>six per cent</u> **(Q35)** of world tea consumption, which is the same as <u>Russia</u> **(Q36)**. Japan, another traditional tea consumer, makes up five per cent. Chinese consumption outstrips these countries with sixteen per cent, but <u>India</u> **(Q37)** is the largest consumer with twenty-three per cent. The rest of the tea consumption across the world is shared around the rest of the world.

Producing tea is a careful process. For optimum taste, the best quality teas are grown at tea gardens at an altitude of five thousand to seven thousand feet above sea level. It begins with plucking, the removal of the right parts from the tea plant, Camellia sinensis. Pluckers are specially trained to only select two leaves and a bud. Plucking is maintained at about seven day intervals. The plucked leaves are collected in baskets, taking care that the leaves are not crushed by overloading. The leaves and buds then need to be withered. During the withering process, the leaf is induced to lose <u>moisture</u> **(Q38)** to prepare it for further processing. Normally this is carried out by spreading tea leaves thinly on troughs through which warm air is circulated by fans. The average length of the withering time depends greatly on the quality of the leaf peculiar to the region where it has been grown.

When satisfactory withering has taken place, the leaf is ready for rolling. This process uses grooved rollers that twist the leaves, break them up and take out the juices. Leaves pass through three to four such rollers, getting reduced in size and their <u>cells</u> **(Q39)** broken up to enable fermentation. Normally the tea ferments or oxidises from sixty to a hundred minutes, depending upon the leaf quality. The character of the tea develops significantly during the fermentation process. The next part of the process is drying. The objective of drying is to arrest fermentation and remove any dampness from the tea. After completion of the drying process, the tea becomes fully black in colour.

The teas are then sorted, graded and packed. The tea is sold at <u>auctions</u> **(Q40)** to traders who then employ tasters to decide how the teas should be blended to create the specific brands or retail requirements.

**That is the end of part four. You will now have half a minute to check your answers.**

*(30 second gap)*

**That is the end of listening test five.**

Made in the USA
Coppell, TX
20 September 2022